The

LOWCOUNTRY
MURDER *of*
GWENDOLYN ELAINE FOGLE

For Peggy + Fraser –
With Best Regards –

The
LOWCOUNTRY
MURDER *of*
GWENDOLYN ELAINE FOGLE

A COLD CASE
SOLVED

LIEUTENANT RITA Y. SHULER,
Retired Special Agent, South Carolina
Law Enforcement Division

'21

THE
History
PRESS

Published by The History Press
Charleston, SC
www.historypress.com

Copyright © 2021 by Rita Y. Shuler
All rights reserved

First published 2021

Manufactured in the United States

ISBN 9781467147002

Library of Congress Control Number: 2020945792

Notice: The information in this book is true and complete to the best of our knowledge. It is offered without guarantee on the part of the author or The History Press. The author and The History Press disclaim all liability in connection with the use of this book.

*This book is dedicated to the memory of Gwendolyn Elaine Fogle
and to her family and loved ones who will forever have her in their hearts.*

What makes cold case investigations so powerful are the families who never give up hope, and the powerful moment when law enforcement FINALLY solves a case and the voice of the victim hasn't been silenced.

—Paula Zahn

CONTENTS

Contents

PREFACE

When I finished writing my third book, *Small-Town Slayings in South Carolina*, I was pretty sure that would be my final one.

I never lost sight, however, that if my last story in the book, "The Unsolved Murder of Gwendolyn Elaine Fogle," should ever be solved, that just might change my mind. In May 2015, I had the honor to team up with Corporal Gean Johnson, investigator with the Walterboro Police Department. We put our heads together, found the missing links and solved the case.

We contribute this to the work of former investigators, the preservation of evidence from the beginning and through the years, today's advanced forensic technology and most importantly, the grace of God.

This is a case that will forever be etched in South Carolina's history and especially in the minds of everyone who knew Gwendolyn Elaine Fogle.

Elaine, we never gave up on you. You were never forgotten. You will forever remain with us.

I chronicle this case with sincere compassion and respect to all concerned. Some segments of interviews, court transcripts and published articles have been edited to facilitate reading.

ACKNOWLEDGEMENTS

First and foremost, my deepest gratitude and thanks to Corporal Gean Johnson, Walterboro Police Department. Without his dedication, passion and persistence to solve Elaine's murder, I would not be writing this sequel and giving it an ending.

My deepest and personal thanks to my forever friend and SLED partner, latent print examiner Tom Darnell, for always being there when I needed his expertise, help, advice or just to talk. There was never a lack of words when we reminisced about the cases we worked together and "getting the bad guy."

My heartfelt appreciation to Eolean Fogle Hughes, Melissa Hughes and the extended Fogle family for their kindness and caring all through the years and for sharing their personal memories of Elaine with me.

Special thanks to my friend Vicky Hall for her motivation and that extra prayer when I really needed it.

To Kathleen Thornley, sincere thanks for your helpful spur-of-the-moment assistance.

Thanks for the assistance of the following:

South Carolina Fourteenth Circuit Solicitor's Office: Solicitor Duffie Stone, Deputy Solicitor Sean Thornton, Retired Assistant Solicitor Steve Knight, Assistant Solicitor Tameaka Legette, the Career Criminal Prosecution Unit, communications director Jeff Kidd and Erinn McGuire, community outreach.

South Carolina Law Enforcement Division: Special Agent Natalie Crosland, AFIS Operator Hayes Baylor, DNA Analyst Laura Hash, Captain Emily Rhinehart, Retired Captain David Caldwell, Mary Perry, Sebrena Matthews and Lorri Johnson.

Walterboro Police Department: Caroline Long, Officer Rusty Davis and Joani Varnadoe.

I am indebted to the *Press and Standard* staff and reporters George Salsberry and Katrena McCall for allowing me to use information from their past publications to help fill in the blanks of some of the progress of the case over the years.

My sincere thanks to the producers and staff of *On the Case with Paula Zahn* on the ID Investigative Channel for their interest in Elaine's case and their excellent work of presenting her story on national television. It will forever honor Elaine's memory. The episode "Twisted Justice" aired in December 2019.

An extra shout-out of thanks to Lindsey Fiesta and Heather Walsh for keeping me informed with the filming and production all along the way. It was an amazing experience.

My very personal thanks to Paula Zahn for her inspirational words to me after my interview: "I see a sequel in the works." Her words stimulated my energy and motivation to write it all down.

To my little parrotlet, Kirbi, thank you, sweet boy, for your cheerful chattering and chirping in the background during my many hours of writing.

My sincere appreciation and thanks to everyone at Arcadia Publishing and The History Press for their guidance, professionalism and personal assistance with the publishing of my books.

1

THE ATTACK

May 27, 1978

Walterboro, South Carolina, is a small Lowcountry town about fifty miles west of Charleston, South Carolina. It is filled with historic charm and overflowing with southern hospitality that some might say is infectious. One of the many charms of small-town living is what lies just up the street and around the corner. Known as the "Front Porch of the Lowcountry," Walterboro's friendly down-home atmosphere captivates visitors as well as all who have made it their home.

On Saturday, May 27, 1978, devastating news hit hard in this Lowcountry town and filled Walterboro residents with intense sadness and horrifying fear. One of their own, twenty-six-year-old Gwendolyn Elaine Fogle, was brutally attacked, sexually assaulted and murdered in her home on South Lemacks Street.

That Saturday evening, Elaine had babysat for her friends Patricia and Bert Utsey. She arrived at their home about 6:45 p.m. She was happy and excited because she was going to visit with her mom and dad the next day to celebrate her mom's birthday, and she was looking forward to seeing her sister, Eolean, and brother-in-law, Larry, who would also be there. Her parents, Myrtis and Wells Fogle, lived in Orangeburg, South Carolina, which is about fifty-five miles from Walterboro.

She left the Utseys' around 11:15 p.m. and told them she was going to stop at the Zippy Mart on her way home, which would have her arriving home around 11:30 p.m.

Elaine's home on Lemacks Street, where she was murdered. *Elaine Fogle case file.*

Elaine's roommate, Nancy Hooker, and friend Billy O'Bryant worked at the J.P. Steven's Company in Walterboro. That Saturday, they had attended an Amway Products Fair in Conway, South Carolina, which is about 150 miles from Walterboro. When they returned home to Walterboro around 1:45 a.m. on Sunday morning, Billy pulled into the driveway to drop off Nancy. As they walked onto the front porch, they noticed the lights on in the house. They both thought it was a little strange that Elaine would be up that late, as she had told them that she was going to visit her parents the next morning.

Using Nancy's key, Billy unlocked the front door, and they walked into a horrendous and shocking scene. They saw Elaine covered in blood, unconscious and partially nude lying on the living room floor in front of the couch. Nancy and Billy became hysterical and immediately rushed to the Walterboro Police Department, which was only about a mile away. Still badly shaken, they told police officers that they could not tell if Elaine was alive or dead, but it appeared that she had been severely beaten and possibly sexually assaulted.

Walterboro police officers immediately responded to the South Lemacks address and checked Elaine's pulse. There was none. EMS arrived at the home shortly afterward and checked Elaine for any vital signs. There were none.

Left: Body location in front of couch. *Elaine Fogle case file.*

Right: End table near front door knocked over during struggle. *Elaine Fogle case file.*

Elaine was lying on her back on top of the hook rug in front of the couch. One foot was partially up on the couch and one foot was on the floor. Her shoes were still on. She was nude from the waist down. Her bra and shirt were pulled up around her neck. Her head and face were covered in blood. There was a metal fire poker wrapped around her neck.

There was a blood trail on the floor right inside the doorway leading to where her body was located on the rug in front of the couch, which indicated that she had been dragged from the doorway to that area during the attack.

Because the front door was locked when Nancy and Billy got home, investigators thought that the attacker might have already been inside the house when Elaine arrived home. When she unlocked the front door and stepped inside, he probably administered his first blow and then locked the door behind her to keep her from escaping. Elaine appeared to have been beaten with any weapons of opportunity that the killer could get his hands on, which included a lamp, a smiley face bank, a walking cane and the metal fire poker.

The entire living room was in total disarray. Items in her home were broken and thrown all around the room. An end table was thrown over against the wall near the front door. Blood was everywhere.

Colleton County pathologist Dr. Frank Trefny and coroner P.J. Maxey were called to the scene. Dr. Trefny photographed the scene and Elaine's body when he arrived. He observed deep contusions and linear abrasions on her hands and knuckles, which he confirmed to be defensive wounds from Elaine's attempts to block blows and fight off her attacker. This indicated that she had put up one hell of a fight. Dr. Trefny's preliminary examination at the scene revealed that Elaine's death was caused by severe head injuries and strangulation from the metal fire poker wrapped around her neck.

The Walterboro Police Department called for assistance from the Colleton County Sheriff's Office.

After checking around the outside of the house, investigators saw that the killer had entered through a rear window by breaking the glass, reaching in, unlocking the window and forcing it up. There were broken pieces of glass on the dining room floor inside the house below the window. There were shoe prints in the sand below all the windows, so it appeared that there were attempts on all three windows to try to gain entry before he succeeded in getting the dining room window open.

Metal fire poker that was around Elaine's neck. *Elaine Fogle case file.*

Broken rear window was the point of entry. *Elaine Fogle case file.*

Broken glass on floor below point of entry. *Elaine Fogle case file.*

Shoe print in sand below rear window. *Elaine Fogle case file.*

Investigators were informed that Elaine worked at a doctor's office, and they considered that since drug activity was prevalent in many areas of the town, the intruder might have broken into the house looking for drugs.

This reinforced the investigator's belief that the killer was inside the house, probably in the process of a burglary when Elaine arrived home. The element of surprise as Elaine opened the door and stepped inside enraged him, and the burglary went wrong. He then started attacking her, and it turned into a sexually motivated attack and murder.

The living room appeared to be the only scene of attack activity. Elaine's roommate's bedroom was ransacked, but there was no sign of attack in that room. Drawers from her dresser were open and rummaged through. Some of her bikini panties were on top of the dresser and in the trash can. Her bed was ruffled, and her little dog was found under her bed, shaking and trembling.

Elaine's car was still parked in the driveway, but her keys were missing. After a thorough search of the entire house, the keys were never found.

Elaine had been living in Walterboro since 1972 and was a medical assistant with Dr. Joseph Flowers, a prominent physician in Walterboro, so she was well known in the town. Word traveled fast of her brutal attack.

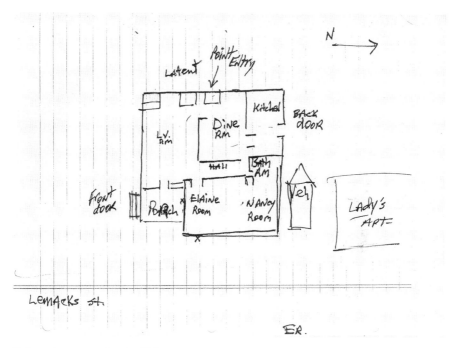

Police crime scene sketch of Elaine's house. *Elaine Fogle case file.*

Dr. Flowers was quickly alerted about Elaine's attack, and he immediately rushed to her house. After learning that Elaine's keys were missing and knowing that she had a key to his office on her key ring, without delay, Dr. Flowers and Billy O'Bryant went to the office and changed the locks on all of the doors.

After speaking to Dr. Flowers, investigators were more confident that the attacker might have known that Elaine worked at his office, and by taking her keys, it would give him entry to Dr. Flowers's office so that he might get access to drugs.

Elaine's bloody jeans were found on the roof of the back porch, so the killer had apparently exited the house by the back door and threw her jeans on the roof as he was leaving.

The South Carolina Law Enforcement Division (SLED) bloodhound team was called in from Columbia, but because of the time that had elapsed since the attack and the amount of foot traffic in and around the scene, the bloodhounds were unable to be of any assistance.

Lieutenant Robert Carter, with the Walterboro Police Department, took charge of the scene and investigation. The scene was photographed and processed for evidence. Much evidence, including fingerprints, palm prints, blood, hairs, clothing and items from the home, were collected and preserved. They would be submitted to the South Carolina Law Enforcement Division Forensic Lab and the Medical University Forensic Lab for further examination.

2.
The Aftermath

Gwendolyn Elaine Fogle

Elaine was born on December 15, 1951, in Orangeburg, South Carolina. After graduating from Orangeburg Calhoun Technical Education Center in 1972, she moved from Orangeburg to Walterboro and worked at Colleton Regional Hospital as a laboratory assistant. She later left the hospital position and accepted a medical assistant position with Dr. Joseph Flowers.

Dr. Flowers described Elaine as a hardworking, diligent girl. "She would go out of her way to help people. I am deeply distraught over her murder," he said. "It is very difficult for me to accept. I don't know of any finer person than Elaine."

Friends shared their personal feelings of knowing Elaine:

> *Elaine became a real part of the community soon after she moved here and made friends easily. She was a dedicated worker, took children to baseball games, and sang in the choir at St. Judes Episcopal Church. She had a cute kind of shyness about her and had the biggest heart. We never heard her say anything unkind about anybody.*
>
> *Elaine was starting to have a lot going for her and recently started taking night classes at Baptist College in Charleston, South Carolina, to pursue her college degree. She had also completed some local art courses. One of her dreams was to become an accomplished artist.*

Gwendolyn Elaine Fogle. *Courtesy of Eolean Fogle Hughes.*

INFORMING ELAINE'S FAMILY

The Walterboro Police Department contacted the Orangeburg Police Department and asked for its assistance in informing Elaine's parents about what had happened. Officer Gene Brant was in the room at the police department when the call came in. He was a friend of the Fogle family and a

Elaine and her parents. *Courtesy of Eolean Fogle Hughes.*

neighbor of Elaine's mom's sister Miriam and her husband, Jimmy. Officer Brant was distraught by the news but wanted to be the one to deliver it to Elaine's parents. He went by Miriam and Jimmy's house first and informed them of the situation. Miriam called their pastor and asked him to go with them to be with Elaine's parents.

Elaine's older sister, Eolean, and her husband, Larry, lived in Whitmire, South Carolina, which is about sixty miles from Orangeburg. She and Larry were also planning to celebrate Elaine and Eolean's mom's birthday that Sunday.

Eolean got off work at about midnight that Saturday night. When she arrived home, Larry told her, "I've got a strange feeling, and I feel like we need to go on down to your Mama and Daddy's tonight."

Eolean agreed, so they packed up and headed to Orangeburg. When they got to her parents, they chitchatted and visited for a little while and then Larry and Mr. Fogle went to bed. Eolean and her mom sat around the kitchen table and talked until about three o'clock in the morning, and then they went to bed. They had been in bed for about thirty minutes when Mr. and Mrs. Fogle were awakened by a knock on their bedroom window and a voice calling out, "Myrtis, it's Miriam. I need you to come to the front door right now!"

Officer Brant, Miriam, Jimmy and their pastor went inside and informed them of what had happened to Elaine. After hearing the news, shocked and distraught, Elaine's mom said, "She was coming to see me on my birthday, today." Then she cried out, "Oh, my God my daughter was murdered on my birthday!"

Consoling themselves as best as they could, they contacted other family members with the news. Eolean, Larry and Mr. and Mrs. Fogle then drove to Walterboro to meet with police officers. Officers told the family that Elaine appeared to have been beaten to death and strangled with a metal fire poker around her neck.

Mr. Fogle got very emotional and upset when they told him about the fire poker wrapped around his daughter's neck. He put his head in his hands and said, "Oh my God, I gave her that fire poker. She kept it next to the front door for her protection."

An autopsy was performed the following morning at the Colleton Regional Hospital in Walterboro. On the following Tuesday, Elaine's funeral service was held at Thompson Funeral Home Chapel in Orangeburg. One of the funeral directors found a single pink rose on his desk with a note that read, "This is for Elaine." The note was not signed.

Elaine was buried at St. George Church Cemetery near Bolen Town, South Carolina, which is just a few miles outside of the town of Orangeburg.

3

THE AUTOPSY

Colleton County pathologist Dr. Frank Trefny performed Elaine's autopsy. He noted in his case summary:

This autopsy is performed at the request of and after due authorization of the coroner of Colleton county in the autopsy room of the Colleton Regional Hospital on May 28, 1978 at approximately 9:00 a.m.

Post mortem examination and autopsy of the body of the deceased, a white female revealed the presence of a black metal fire poker around the neck. It took two people to remove the poker from the neck. When removed, this leaves an abrasion, and a pattern injury with crosshatching which has the same pattern trait as the handle of the fire poker. Multiple contusions, abrasions and lacerations are present about the face and head. The facial features are distorted. A contusion over the right forehead shows the same crosshatched pattern as the handle of the fire poker. Contusions and linear abrasions are present on the right hand. The abrasions on the right hand are a slightly crosshatch pattern similar to, but lighter in color than those on the neck and forehead. There are abrasions, contusions and small lacerations over the knuckles on the right hand. The injuries are classified as defense wounds resulting from repeated attempts, of the deceased to defend herself from her attacker. Large amounts of blood are also present on both hands. Patterned injures in the form of abrasions are present on the abdomen. Examination of the trunk reveals multiple semi-elliptical abrasions on the lower portion of the right rib cage and onto the right upper quadrant of the abdomen. A similar configuration is seen on a piece of broken pottery in the same room of death.

On the abdomen area, there is a pattern in blood that has a sort of ribbed shape. There is a slightly ribbed pattern in blood present on the left arm, resembling the ribbed pattern on the abdomen.

The blood of the deceased, Elaine Fogle is typed and documented as O positive.

Scrapings are removed from beneath the fingernails of each hand which include soft tissue and skin. The skin shows a slight amount of pigment present.

The materials obtained beneath the fingernails of the deceased are placed in appropriately labeled containers and deferred to the Histology Laboratory of the Medical University of South Carolina (MUSC).

Examination of vaginal and rectal smears taken from Elaine's body at autopsy revealed the presence of large numbers of spermatozoa. Examination of oral smears revealed no spermatozoa.

The finding of large amount of spermatozoa present indicates the deceased had been sexually assaulted. The smears of spermatozoa present are placed in appropriate labeled containers.

The pubic hair is combed and pubic hair is also removed from the skin and placed in appropriately labeled containers.

Based on the clinical history and the post mortem examination and autopsy findings, Dr. Trefny's final opinion reflected that the cause of death was asphyxiation due to the presence of a metal fire poker about the neck. The manner of death was homicide.

After final review of the autopsy and autopsy photographs, Dr. Trefny surmised that the crosshatching patterns on Elaine's neck and forehead were made by the spring handle on the fire poker during the attack. The same crosshatch pattern visible on her right hand and left arm were also from the spring handle of the fire poker. This confirmed that Elaine had been struck multiple times with the fire poker before it was wrapped around her neck, which ended in her death.

On May 30, 1978, the following items removed from Elaine's body at autopsy were transferred to Lieutenant R.C. Carter, Walterboro Police Department, by Dr. Trefny:

1. Combings, pubic hair
2. Pubic hair pulled from skin

3. Fingernail scrapings, left hand
4. Fingernail scrapings, right hand
5. Black metal poker in plastic bag

That same day, the fingernail scrapings from Elaine's right and left hands were transferred to the Medical University of South Carolina by Lieutenant Bob Carter and were signed over to forensic pathologist Dr. Sandra Conradi for her expert evaluation.

4.

INVESTIGATION

Information and an update of the ongoing investigation ran in the June 1, 1978 edition of the Walterboro newspaper, the *Press and Standard*. The front-page headline read "Police Seek Woman's Murderer."

Law enforcement officials are seeking an unknown assailant who brutally murdered Walterboro resident Gwendolyn Elaine Fogle on Saturday, May 27.

Walterboro Public Safety Director, Ken Davis reported that she was attacked as she entered her home at 210 S. Lemacks Street that evening sometime around 11:30 p.m. Her home is just across from the Colleton Regional Hospital which is normally a tranquil neighborhood.

Elaine had apparently struggled with her assailant and may have inflicted scratches or other marks on his body. Director Davis is asking anyone who had observed any black or white male with scratches, cuts or bruises on his body to call the Walterboro Police Department or Colleton County Sheriff's Office. Any person with information will be kept anonymous.

Evidence has been collected from the scene and is being processed by the South Carolina Law Enforcement Division (SLED) and the Medical University of South Carolina. The first lab reports are expected as soon as in the next few days. Davis declined to elaborate further on the evidence stating that "We don't want to disclose our leads until they're fully developed. It might hamper the investigation."

1877 Serving Colleton County For 101 Years 1978

15¢
Copy

The Press and Standard

15¢
Copy

VOL. 101, NO. 31   3 Sections   WALTERBORO, S. C. 29488, THURSDAY, JUNE 1, 1978   40 Pages   1-A

Police Seek Woman's Murderer

Courtesy of the Press and Standard.

Several suspects have been questioned, based on their previous records, but all has since been eliminated as suspects.

A $1,000 reward has been offered by a Walterboro resident to anyone furnishing information that might lead to the arrest and conviction of the assailant, but far more important than any monetary consideration is the need to get a dangerous man off the street.

The Colleton County Medical Auxiliary along with friends of Elaine have started an Elaine Fogle Scholarship for Walterboro area high school students; $250 will be awarded annually to a graduate of any school in Colleton County to further their pursuit of an education in the allied health careers field.

"This investigation will remain on the front burner, and we will be working on it every day."

5

SOUTH CAROLINA LAW ENFORCEMENT DIVISION (SLED)

The South Carolina Law Enforcement Division (SLED) is a state-level law enforcement and investigative agency with statewide jurisdiction and investigative services. SLED provides technical services and manpower assistance to local, state and federal entities throughout the state upon request by the law enforcement agency in charge of the investigation. The SLED Forensics Lab provides all law enforcement agencies in the state of South Carolina with expert testing and analysis of forensic evidence, as requested.

Walterboro Police Department did not request the assistance of the South Carolina Law Enforcement Division's Crime Scene Unit in the early morning hours of Elaine's investigation on May 28, 1978. The crime scene was photographed and processed by the Walterboro Police Department investigators. Photographs taken at a crime scene are critical to an investigation to properly document the exact conditions at the scene precisely how the assailant left it. After the crime scene was photographed, Walterboro investigators documented, collected and preserved evidence from the scene.

Elaine's case information, evidence from the crime scene and the rolls of 35-millimeter film taken at the site were submitted to the SLED Forensics Lab on Tuesday, May 30, 1978. In 1978, digital photography did not exist. The rolls of film had to be manually developed and printed in the lab. It was a dip-and-dunk process, using tanks and a photo developer solution. Photographic prints were then printed from the processed negatives.

Shuler working with SLED crime scene photos. *Author collection.*

As supervisor of the SLED Forensics Photography Lab, it was my job to take charge of all of the photographs from agencies that submitted them to SLED. A crime scene is totally preserved with photographs, as they are the true documentation. They can be stored indefinitely and retrieved at any time to assist in investigations.

In 1978, the filing system in the photography lab was a brown manila envelope that included photo work requests, negatives and photographs. The case envelope was then filed in the drawer of a file cabinet in the photography lab. With all the technology of the digital era, the way of preserving the evidence and filing back then would now be referred to as the old-school method.

On May 30, 1978, when Elaine's case came across my desk, I had been with SLED for seven months. I processed the rolls of film from the crime scene and printed photographs from the negatives.

A strange sensitivity and visual moment came over me as I viewed the photographs. I noticed that Elaine and I had very similar taste in dress. In the photos, her shirt that was pulled up around her neck was a short sleeved, striped, three-button shirt that we called a "rugger" back then. I sometimes wore the same kind. Her jeans were missing, but strangely, both of her shoes were still on. Her shoes were Sperry Top-Sider loafers, just like I wore. She

Corn-sheller and broken items in room of attack. *Elaine Fogle case file.*

had personal items in her home that I had in my home—country things, a butter churn, stone jugs and a hand-operated corn sheller.

One of the investigators asked me, "What is a corn sheller?" Having grown up on a farm, I explained that it was a hand-operated tool with hard metal spikes used to shell dried corn off the cob to be used to feed the animals.

He commented, "I would tend to say not many people would have a corn sheller in their home." I would have to agree with that, and again, that just strengthened the feeling of a connection to Elaine. We both had a country corn sheller in our home.

My biggest shock was when I viewed the metal fire poker around her neck. I had exactly the same kind of fire poker on my fireplace in my home.

Elaine and I were close to the same age, and we were both born and raised in Orangeburg County, South Carolina. After high school, she and I both pursued careers in the medical field. Elaine was a certified laboratory technologist. I was a registered X-ray technologist. She left Orangeburg and relocated to Walterboro to work at the Colleton County Regional Hospital. I left Orangeburg County and continued my profession as X-ray technologist for thirteen years in Columbia, South Carolina, before starting my law enforcement career with SLED in 1977. Elaine's case undeniably hit home with me, to a point that I had an eerie feeling of a personal connection with her.

Walterboro investigators submitted evidence they had collected at the crime scene, as well as the lifts of the palm prints and fingerprints found at the scene, to the SLED Latent Print Lab. SLED latent print examiners transferred the lifts of the palm prints and fingerprints to the photography lab to be photographed.

The equipment in the photography lab setup made it possible to bring out more details of the prints by using controlled conditions such as lighting, different ranges of film and more sophisticated cameras. Larger format cameras were used so that an exact size (1:1) image could be captured. This is of upmost importance when using a photograph of a fingerprint, palm print, and footprint from the scene to compare to a known print of a suspect. The prints have to be the same size as the known print of the suspect.

Lighting is extremely critical when photographing crucial evidence. How much light, the direction of light and how it falls on the evidence are major factors in bringing out fine details that are sometimes not visible with normal viewing. Too much light or too little light can also cause fine details to be lost. There is also a possibility that the final developed negative would reveal even more detailed definition than what is seen through the lens of the camera.

The latent fingerprints, palm prints and shoe prints from Elaine's case were photographed and printed 1:1. When SLED latent print examiners viewed the crime scene photos of Elaine's scene, they observed the ribbed shape pattern on her abdomen and left arm that had also been noted on her autopsy report. It appeared to be a partial bloody shoe print. The

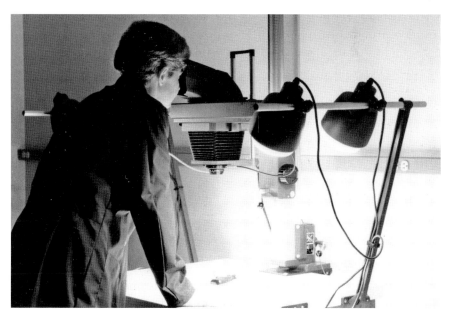

Shuler photographing evidence in SLED photography lab. *Author's collection.*

bloody print had similarities with the shoe print found on the ground below the back windows of Elaine's home at the point of entry, which probably belonged to the killer.

While in the process of the attack, he most likely stepped in blood that was present all over the living room floor, and then it transferred to the outsole of his shoe. At some point, his bloody shoe came in contact with Elaine's abdomen area and arm, leaving the partial bloody impression of the shoe outsole. A thought was that he might have been using his foot to hold her body down while wrapping the fire poker around her neck, and blood on the outsole of his shoe transferred to Elaine's abdomen and arm, leaving the partial pattern.

Investigators know that one of the most important pieces of evidence that might be left by a suspect at a crime scene is a palm print, fingerprint, footprint or shoe print in the victim's blood. This places the suspect at the scene, touching or making contact with the victim's blood.

With no suspects and no shoes to compare to the print outside the window or the bloody pattern on Elaine's abdomen, this was of no help to the investigation at this point. As the investigation continued, Walterboro periodically submitted inked palm prints and fingerprint impressions of possible suspects to the SLED Latent Print Lab to be compared to the latent prints found at the scene.

Unfortunately, none yielded a match to any of the prints from the scene.

6.

A SUSPECT

T he cloud of fear continued to hover over Walterboro. Elaine's attack and brutal murder was the main topic of conversation everywhere. Women were afraid to go out or stay home alone. Men feared for their families.

As early as the morning of Elaine's attack, Walterboro investigators had focused on a person of interest. Ronald Allen, a twenty-three-year-old White male, lived in a trailer with his wife and child right around the corner from Elaine, and investigators had run-ins with him in the past.

Allen was a shade tree mechanic and had a chain hoist on a tree in his backyard to hang an engine. He had a workout bench in his front yard and worked out every day. He was very strong and muscular, six feet tall and 250 pounds. Investigators thought that he would definitely be strong enough to wrap the fire poker around Elaine's neck. Also, as he lived in close proximity of Elaine, it would be an easy crime of opportunity for him to enter Elaine's home.

Investigators talked to Ron Allen and his wife, Fran, the morning after Elaine's murder. They said they did not know Elaine, even though she lived right down the street from them. When Ron asked why they were questioning him, one investigator stated that the SLED dogs led them to their trailer.

Fran told investigators to take a look at the inside of the trailer they lived in because it was small. She said that Ron slept on the wall side of the bed, and if he had gotten out of bed that night, she would have known because he would have crawled across her.

Fran also told one of the investigators that while she was getting dressed for work that morning, she looked out of the window and saw a Black man with no shirt on standing in their backyard at the water faucet washing his chest and face.

Investigators asked Ron if he smoked pot or did acid or drugs. He emphatically replied, "Yes, when I can get it from my friends, but I did not kill that girl, and I had nothing to do with whatever happened."

Investigators collected all of Ron's shoes and compared the outsoles to the shoe prints found on the ground below the windows at the point of entry to Elaine's house. None of the outsoles of his shoes were a match to the shoe prints.

At this point, there was nothing substantial to link Ron Allen to Elaine's murder, but investigators had already formed a strong fixation on him. Ron's background check showed that he came from a large family of eleven children, and his father died at a young age. His juvenile record reflected that he had stolen a police car in Michigan that ended in a chase into Ohio, where he was shot in the neck when the chase ended. He went to prison and was released at the age of twenty-one.

He enlisted in the army for a brief period, around 1976–77, but was soon discharged because of his criminal record. Allen's passion was cars, and he loved working on them. He could actually pick up the front of a car by himself. He was known to steal tools from his job at BP Motors and other places where he did mechanic work. Over the years, a history of violence, assaults, burglaries and numerous DUI arrests followed Ronald Allen. All of this just added to investigators' persistent focus on Ronald Allen.

This information of a potential suspect was not released to the public, but Walterboro was a small town, so it didn't take long for on-the-street rumors to begin flying around with a vengeance. Talk that a suspect had been captured spread throughout the town, putting everyone in a frenzy.

Walterboro Police had the *Press and Standard* run an article to inform the public that the rumors of a suspect being captured in Elaine's case were simply not true, and the misinformation was creating confusion and anxiety among residents. The article urged anyone who heard apparently reasonable stories to avoid spreading them further and to call the Walterboro Police Department.

With the case still ongoing, information that could be released to the public was very limited, as it could jeopardize the investigation.

7

INVESTIGATION CONTINUES

Colleton County sheriff John Seigler contacted Colleton County resident SLED agent Chad Caldwell for his assistance with Elaine's investigation. SLED agents Lieutenant Leonard Kizer, Lieutenant Jack Kemmerlin and Special Agent L.C. Knight were also assigned to assist Lieutenant Bob Carter and Detective Earl Fowler of the Walterboro Police Department.

Elaine's acquaintances, boyfriend and close friends were interviewed.

Approximately forty items of evidence from the scene were submitted to the SLED chemistry lab to be analyzed. The items included Elaine's clothing, blood and hair from the house, as well as some red fibers that were near her body. Blood type, semen, hair and fiber analysis were requested on the items.

On June 8, 1978, SLED chemistry analyst John Barron submitted a report to the Walterboro Police Department. Results of all of the blood evidence submitted was typed as O positive, which Dr. Trefny had already confirmed at the autopsy as being Elaine's blood type. Of course, there was always the possibility that the killer's blood type could also be O positive. In 1978, blood could only be typed and grouped.

The hair that was submitted was found to be all Caucasian, except for two hair samples that were found to be white animal hair. Red fibers that were submitted were found to be of unknown origin.

Reports showed that nothing indicative of semen were found on any of the items that had been submitted. The semen swabs that Dr. Trefny collected from Elaine's body at autopsy had not yet been submitted to the SLED lab. That brought up the question, "Where are the vials that contain the semen?"

Documents show that it wasn't until July 5, 1978, that SLED agent Chad Caldwell met with Dr. Trefny and the semen swabs were transferred to Agent Caldwell to be submitted to the SLED chemistry lab for analysis. Agent Caldwell signed as receiving the following from Dr. Trefny on that date, July 5, 1978:

(a) one glass vial containing vaginal smear from Elaine Fogle
(b) one glass vial containing rectal smear from Elaine Fogle
(c) one glass vial containing oral smear from Elaine Fogle

At this point, nothing conclusive had been returned from the crime scene evidence that had been submitted to SLED and the Medical University of South Carolina that might lead to a suspect. This information did not stop the investigation from going on. All tips or information that came forward were checked out as possibly being related to Elaine's murder.

Several weeks after the murder, a concerned former employer of potential suspect Ron Allen contacted police. He told them that Ron had stopped working for him about a month before Elaine was murdered, but on the day before Elaine was murdered, Ron came into his shop. He looked at a dark green Ford Gran Torino with the intention of purchasing it. Ron left, telling his former employer that he would get back to him. The next day, the employer said he started hearing the news about Elaine's murder. He stated that when he arrived at his lot the next morning, the Gran Torino was not on the lot, and he reported the car missing.

Around four to six weeks later, a sheriff from Cookeville, Tennessee, contacted the Walterboro Police Department and informed them they had located the vehicle. It had been in the possession of Ronald Allen. It had bald tires and was full of beer cans. This strengthened the investigators' obsession with Ronald Allen, but still, it was nothing that could be used to warrant an arrest.

Even though investigators kept their eye on Ron Allen as the main suspect, they continued checking out people who were arrested in the area on any charges. Their fingerprints and palm prints were submitted to SLED and checked with the prints in Elaine's case file at SLED. None were a match.

Possible suspects based on previous records and any other persons of interest who might furnish information continued to be questioned. Some suspects were polygraphed at SLED, but all results showed they were unlikely to be related to Elaine's death.

In September 1978, the *Press and Standard* ran an update of the status of the investigation.

> *Elaine Fogle's assault and murder remains a mystery, but law enforcement officials indicate that the case is still being pursued actively.*
>
> *Walterboro Police Chief Ken Davis said, "We have not put the case on a back burner and we won't. It is still very active, and something is done on it every day. We feel confident that we're going to get him, but we can't put a timetable on it at this time."*
>
> *Lt. Bob Carter, chief investigator on the case reported that all persons arrested in the area are being checked out, as well as persons in other cities and states.*
>
> *Both officers have indicated that nothing conclusive has come out of the crime scene evidence that is still being processed at SLED and the Medical University of South Carolina.*

From day one of Elaine's murder, her family never gave up hope that the murderer would be found. Elaine's mother even contacted a psychic, Mary Green, in Columbia, South Carolina. Green said it had something to do with drugs, and they really didn't want Elaine, but that's why she was killed. She took the tape to investigators, but they told her they did not believe in that kind of stuff. Elaine's mother also asked the police if Elaine's story could be run on the TV series *Unsolved Mysteries*, and they told her that wouldn't help.

After hitting some dead ends with investigators, Elaine's parents began their own investigation along with the help of some other family members.

Elaine's cousin Wanda and her husband, David Simpson, were newlyweds. David had just finished law school and started a job with the City of Walterboro. They moved to Walterboro and had hopes that with David's law background he might be able to assist with Elaine's case. David met with the Walterboro police chief, and the chief was very cordial and encouraging and said he would let David know if he could be of any assistance. David returned to the police station periodically week after week, but investigators had little to tell him and seemed to make it clear that there was nothing he could do to help them.

Wanda said, "This deepened our fear, and it became scary. We suspected everyone in town. Always looking over our shoulders and wondering, is it him, is it him?"

But Elaine's family didn't stop. They continued to contact Walterboro Police Department to try to find out what was going on with the case, only to be told that there was nothing new. This just added to their sadness and pain. They even wondered, "Has Elaine been forgotten?" Days and months passed with no new breaks in the case.

Advanced Training

October 1979

In October 1979, after completing a ten-week basic police training course at the South Carolina Criminal Justice Academy, I was certified as a law enforcement officer with South Carolina and gained the title of special agent with SLED.

This opened the door for specialized assignments, other than forensic photographer, such as security assignments, crowd control, extradition duties and working with victims and witnesses to compose facial composites of offenders. I did a little bit of everything, especially when a female was needed.

Through the years, I attended many miscellaneous law enforcement in-service classes relating to all areas of law enforcement. Three of these were advanced forensic photography courses at the FBI Academy in Quantico, Virginia. After my training at the FBI Academy, I incorporated many of the photography procedures and techniques in the SLED photography lab, which proved to be extremely advantageous with investigations and working with the evidence.

Even though I had gained the title of special agent, my heart still remained with the forensic photography lab and assisting with crime scene investigations. Working with the evidence and assisting investigators with putting the pieces together to get the bad guy off the street was a passion for me. I felt that every piece of evidence I worked with was helping the victims and their loved ones.

Some cases do become personal, and they just never leave you.

Do they bother you? Yes, they do.

Do you take them home? Yes, you do.

Do they keep you awake at night? Yes, they do.

Elaine's case was undeniably one of these for me. It remained at the forefront of my mind, and I would periodically check on updates and the status of the investigation. Again, days, months and years passed with no suspects or arrests. Gwendolyn Elaine Fogle's murder had now become Walterboro Police Department's number one cold case.

New Suspects

Six Years after the Murder, March 1984

In March 1984, investigators thought they might finally have the break they had been waiting years for.

Two inmates asked to talk to officers because they wanted to tell them that they knew something about the murder and assault of a nurse named Elaine in Walterboro back in 1978. At first, they both hinted that they had done it and then threw out several names of acquaintances who had told them they killed Elaine. They even got to the point of bragging about it.

Investigators knew that it is not unusual for people to talk themselves up while in prison just to look big or possibly get a break on their sentences.

In conversation with the inmates, the investigators did become more concerned when the inmates relayed pertinent details of Elaine's attack that night, some they believed only the killer would know about, but they figured that the inmates could have just heard talk and rumors on the street. They even could have heard the killer running his mouth about the murder.

Thorough background and up-to-date checks were done on the inmates and on the people whose names they gave up in the interviews. Nothing substantial was found to link any of them to Elaine's murder. Even so, investigators remained skeptical, keeping all of these names high on the list of persons of interest. All documentation of communication with these inmates was recorded and placed in Elaine Fogle's case file.

8.

CASE CLOSED

Seven Years after the Murder, July 1985

In July 1985, SLED lieutenant Chad Caldwell filed the following status report in Elaine Fogle's investigative file:

No further information or new leads have developed in this investigation. Therefore, this investigator is closing the investigation until new information surfaces. As the need arises the case will be reopened. This case is closed.

9.
ADVANCED FORENSIC TECHNOLOGY

Eleven Years after the Murder, August 1989

Around 1989, advancements in forensic technology started to be used in criminal investigations. SLED established a Behavioral Science Profiling Unit, which could assist in the investigation and the hope of identifying the responsible party based on the crime scene analysis, investigative psychology and behavioral science.

SLED behavioral profiler captain David Caldwell was requested to review Elaine's case file and provide a profile of a possible suspect. Captain Caldwell consulted with the FBI Behavioral Science Unit in Quantico, Virginia, to assist with the profile. Captain Caldwell's notes reflect:

> *This description of the offender consists of best estimates and are not 100% accurate.*
> - *White male (based more on forensics than behavior)*
> - *Age: 24–30*
> - *Married*
> - *Extremely strong to be able to bend fire poker around her neck*
> - *Probably lived close to scene (likely to have walked)*
> - *May have seen victim and roommate outside at home at some point*
> - *Excessive drinking. May have been drinking prior to the crime and/or using marijuana*
> - *Local arrests for assault*
> - *Problems with women*

- *He has a problem with authority. Elaine fought back. He couldn't handle that.*
- *He did not go to the funeral and within a few months that followed he might have left town.*
- *Wherever he is, he has almost certainly come to the attention of law enforcement for something and has spent part of his life over the last eleven years in and out of jail.*

Also documented in Caldwell's report were his miscelleous notes of findings at the crime scene:

- *Forced entry though rear window.*
- *Weapons of opportunity were used in attack*
- *Fire poker around Elaine's neck belonged by door near corn sheller*
- *Elaine had defense wounds to hands*
- *Living room is only scene of attack activity*
- *"Old lady" type panties on couch*
- *Roommate's room was ransacked: drawers open, bed ruffled, "bikini-type" panties in trash can and on chest*
- *Elaine's car keys missing, but car still in driveway*
- *Elaine's bloody jeans on roof at point of exit*
- *Semen from Elaine's body found at autopsy*
- *Fire poker required two persons to loosen at autopsy*

Even though the main suspect, Ron Allen, had long since moved away from Walterboro, investigators still remained focused on him. This updated profile once again put him at the top of the list for Elaine's murder.

In 1978, when Elaine's murder happened, *DNA* were just three letters of the alphabet. Around 1989, DNA (Deoxyribonucleic acid) profiling was starting to be used in criminal investigations. DNA is the molecule that contains genetic information and is found in body cells and body fluids. It is inherited from both parents. You get half from your mother and half from your father.

That makes an individual's DNA his or her own genetic fingerprint. I also like to think of it as maybe God's personal barcode for someone. No two people have the same DNA, except for identical twins. This results when the single fertilized egg splits into two genetically identical eggs containing matching chromosomes.

DNA profiling could now be used in criminal investigations, comparing suspects' DNA profiles to DNA evidence collected at a crime scene to assess the likelihood of their involvement in the crime. By comparing a DNA profile generated from any type of biological evidence found at the scene of a crime to a known DNA sample obtained from a suspect, an analyst can determine whether the evidence found at the crime scene belongs to that individual.

DNA databases were not yet available, so a standard sample from body fluids of a suspect would be needed to perform a comparison match to DNA collected from evidence at the crime scene or from the victim's body. Automated fingerprint databases were not yet available, but fingerprints, palm prints and footprints from a crime scene could be identifiable if compared to the known prints of the suspect.

The original evidence from Elaine's crime scene was still preserved and on file at Walterboro Police Department, but with no suspects, the new forensic technology offered no assistance to the investigation at this point.

Elaine's family continued to try to stay in contact with investigators for updates on Elaine's investigation, only to be told, "There is nothing new."

It remained a cold case on the shelf in the evidence room. Time is no friend to a cold case. Evidence might deteriorate. Witnesses might no longer be available, or even worse, they might have died, but a cold case never dies; it's just sleeping, waiting for investigators to get back on it and find the link to dig out the truth. There is always hope that one day that link will be found.

10.

A Bizarre Event

Thirteen Years after the Murder, November 1991

Elaine's family continued to try to communicate with the Walterboro Police Department to gain any information they could on the progress of the investigation.

Elaine's daddy died two years after she was murdered. The family will always believe that he grieved himself to death. He was bothered every day of his life after Elaine was killed that he had given Elaine that fire poker. Elaine's mother, at this point sixty-five years old, continued to live alone in Orangeburg, South Carolina, on Old St. Matthews Road.

Thirteen years after Elaine's murder, in November 1991, around midnight on a Friday night, Mrs. Fogle heard a voice outside her house and got up to see if everything was all right. She looked out of the window and saw a Black man in her yard. The man saw her at the window and yelled, "Do you have a gun in there?" She told him that she did, and he yelled back, "I've got one too."

Mrs. Fogle ran to the phone, but the man had cut the wires on the outside, and the phone was dead. The man kicked in the door, ran inside and grabbed Mrs. Fogle. He started hitting her with his fists and a stick, threw her down on the floor and kept hitting her. Mrs. Fogle said he threatened to rape her, but she told him she had AIDS. With that, he left her alone and went through the house and stole five dollars and some of her costume jewelry.

As he was leaving, he yelled, "If you come out of the house, I'll be waiting in the yard and kill you."

Mrs. Fogle stayed huddled in the house until around 9:30 a.m. Knowing her niece drove by her house around that time every day on her way to work, she went outside and flagged her down when she drove by. They went to the Orangeburg County Sheriff's Department for help and reported the incident.

Mrs. Fogle's attacker was never found.

She would say over the years how she knew some of the torture that Elaine might had suffered at the hands of her killer. She also wondered every day after the attack if that might have been the same man that killed Elaine.

Mrs. Fogle died in her sleep in 1999. The physician who examined her body said, "Looks like she just went to sleep and forgot to wake up."

The family knew that Elaine's parents never got over losing Elaine and that her killer was never found. They lived every day with hope that her murder would be solved, and they held on to that hope. Even though Elaine's parents both died without justice for their daughter, the family felt that they were now finally at peace, and they were with their beloved Elaine again. Mr. and Mrs. Fogle were buried next to Elaine at St. George Church Cemetery near Bolen Town, South Carolina.

After Mr. and Mrs. Fogle's deaths, the family continued their attempts to communicate with Walterboro Police Department and SLED about any progress on the case. Once again, years passed with no new progress and no arrests.

11.

A DREAM OF WRITING

Twenty-Three Years after the Murder, October 2001

Thousands of cases came across my desk during my amazing career with SLED, and I learned that justice could become very personal at times. Evil people are always out there doing evil things. Although each case was different, there was always one major factor that was always the same: every case deserves an ending that would bring the offender to justice. Although that is the ideal, it doesn't always happen. Cases go cold. People vanish without a trace and are still missing. It takes dedicated investigators staying on the case and never giving up hope that the missing link will finally be uncovered to solve the case.

Despite the intensity of my career sometimes taking me into dark places, I came to know how much it means to the victims' families, for someone just to listen, care and let them know that their loved ones are not forgotten.

On October 1, 2001, I retired from an amazing and rewarding career with SLED, not because I didn't love my work, but because I could retire and wanted to pursue another dream of mine: writing. In the mid-1980s, I faithfully watched the TV series *Murder She Wrote*. The episodes followed mystery writer and amateur detective Jessica Fletcher, a down-to-earth middle-aged lady. I got hooked and thought, "I just might do that one day."

While at SLED, I was requested by community groups, organizations and schools to speak about my work and the importance of forensic photography and evidence in solving cases, which added a boost for me to think about one day writing about some of my cases. During a memorable moment after one of my lectures at a middle school, the teacher asked his class, "Don't y'all think Lieutenant Shuler needs to write a book?"

I was humbled and smiled and said, "Thank you, but I can't write. English wasn't one of my best subjects in school."

As the students were leaving the room, one little guy looked up at me with his puppy dog eyes and said, "Lieutenant Shuler, you know if you can say it, you can write it." Oh, the innocence of youth back then. I never forgot his words.

That day I'd been thinking about had come, and I began to chronicle some South Carolina true crime cases that I worked on during my tenure at SLED. I would bring in the investigations and how they were solved by the work of dedicated investigators, along with physical evidence. I also included several cases that were still unsolved. Solved or unsolved, by putting the stories down in writing, the innocent lives that were so ruthlessly taken by the vicious acts of others would never be forgotten.

Now that advanced technology with DNA and fingerprints was firing up and starting to be used more and more in criminal investigations, it gave hope to unsolved cases by bringing them back into the eyes of investigators and the public. In the mid-90s, the Combined DNA Index System (CODIS) database setup started, and every day, new entries of arrestees would be entered into the CODIS database, so it continued to grow. A DNA profile from crime scene evidence could now be entered into the CODIS database to check for a match to someone's profile already in CODIS.

Also in the mid-90s, the Automatic Fingerprint Identification System (AFIS) setup began. Fingerprints from arrestees were now being entered into the AFIS database. Fingerprints from the crime scene could be entered in the AFIS database to check for a possible match of someone's print already in AFIS.

After retirement, I was no longer active in an official capacity of law enforcement, so obtaining official records of the cases that I chronicled in my book would have to be acquired under the Freedom of Information Act (FOIA) of South Carolina.

This would be limited, as the case had to be totally adjudicated for the official files to be released through FOIA. The FOIA information could include official case files and documents, court transcripts and information presented at trial. Any public information released from newspapers, websites or any news media coverage document could also be included with permission from the source. My personal thoughts and memories of working with the cases and with family members could also be included.

I pursued the status of Elaine's case, but being retired limited me to what Walterboro Police Department and SLED could share with me. One thing I did know for sure was that Elaine's murder was still unsolved.

12

WALTERBORO POLICE DEPARTMENT AND SLED REOPEN CASE

Twenty-Four Years after the Murder, July 2002

Elaine's killer was cold and savage and, to this point, had gotten away with it. Odds are that he certainly could have committed other crimes after Elaine's attack. Investigators were hoping that if he had been arrested on other charges, his DNA and fingerprints might now be in the CODIS and AFIS databases.

On July 9, 2002, Colleton County sheriff Allan Beach contacted SLED chief Robert Stewart to ask for SLED's assistance in reopening the 1978 murder case of Elaine Fogle. Beach informed Chief Stewart that Elaine's case was still on the minds of citizens of Walterboro because of its brutality and their love for Elaine.

Sheriff Beach said it was never solved, but some new information had surfaced that needed to be checked. He thought the case needed a fresh approach. He was aware that Walterboro Police Department had the case files, and it was possible that SLED had some evidence in its forensic lab.

Chief Stewart assigned SLED special agent Travis Avant to assist. Agent Avant formed an investigative team, which included Walterboro Police Department investigator Robert Carter, who was the primary investigator originally assigned to the case in 1978, and other law enforcement officers with Walterboro Police Department, Colleton County Sheriff's Office and SLED.

Investigators were aware that almost two and a half decades had passed, so there would be obstacles they might still face, but with new advancements in DNA and fingerprint technology, they were optimistic that Elaine's case might now be solved. They were confident that reexamination of the case evidence could possibly render a DNA profile of Elaine's murderer. A DNA standard from Elaine would also be needed, and that could be acquired from the vials of blood collected from Elaine at her autopsy.

Agent Avant's review of the case files indicated that an enormous amount of evidence was gathered at the crime scene in May 1978. Some evidence was submitted to the Medical University of South Carolina forensic pathology lab and some to the SLED forensic lab shortly after the murder. Some of the suspects in 1978 remained at the top of the list, so a DNA sample would need to be obtained from them.

Ronald Allen, the primary suspect, had been gone from the Walterboro area for decades, but investigators remained strongly focused on him as the person who murdered Elaine. Agent Avant immediately set out to locate Ronald Allen and found an address for him in Baxter, Tennessee. He contacted Special Agent Bob Krofssik with the Tennessee Bureau of Investigation (TBI) and briefed him on Elaine's case. He asked for Agent Krofssik's assistance to possibly meet with Ronald Allen and obtain a DNA sample.

Agent Krofssik offered his assistance but said there might be a problem of collecting a DNA sample because Ronald Allen had passed away a few days before and was already buried. He would check with Dr. Sullivan Smith at the Cookeville Regional Hospital, where Allen's autopsy was performed to check on any information and records that he might have available.

Then Agent Krofssik called Agent Avant back with good news. Dr. Smith had drawn two vials of blood from Ronald Allen for drug testing during the autopsy because at that time Allen's cause of death was still pending.

Both vials of blood were transferred to Putnam County EMS director Randy Porter to forward to the TBI crime lab for drug screening. Agent Krofssik made contact with Director Porter and briefed him on Elaine's unsolved murder. Krofssik advised him that SLED needed to obtain a DNA sample from Ron Allen to assist in the investigation.

Director Porter allowed one vial of Ronald Allen's blood to be transferred to SLED agent Avant. Surely, this was a hand to God moment. The blood sample would provide a full DNA profile of Ronald Allen. This could now possibly identify or eliminate Ronald Allen as a suspect.

On August 19, 2002, Agent Avant and Lieutenant Jack Watson with the Colleton County Sheriff's Office traveled to Tennessee to pick up the vial of blood collected from Ronald Allen.

During that time, interviews were conducted with Ronald Allen's brothers, Glenn, Eddie and Gary. Glenn and Eddie voluntarily provided information to officers, telling them that Ronald had not been working for a long time. He had been depressed, was taking pills by the handful for pain from an injury and had been on drugs for years. He could get pretty wild and got into a lot of fights. Ronald had hit Glenn in the neck with a steel bar and almost killed him, and he tried to bite off Eddie's ear.

He had moved back to Tennessee from South Carolina after he divorced his wife, Fran. He never talked much about his time in South Carolina, and he never indicated that he was ever in trouble in South Carolina or had hurt anyone.

Ronald's brother Gary lived out of state and had returned to Tennessee for Ronald's funeral. Gary informed the officers that Ronald had lived with him in Ohio for a short while. When asked if Ronald ever mentioned being involved in a murder in South Carolina, Gary stated that Ronald did mention a time when he was a suspect for a murder in Walterboro, South Carolina, but he never discussed the details.

Ronald had been staying with Glenn in Tennessee before his death. Glenn gave verbal consent to investigators to look in Ronald's room. One brown work boot and one white tennis shoe belonging to Ronald were collected with the consent of Glenn Allen. An interesting find during the search of one of Ronald's dresser drawers were several *Walterboro Press and Standard* newspaper articles from 1978 on Elaine's murder. Investigators kept this in mind, as they knew that murderers sometimes like to keep trophies from their crimes.

On August 23, 2002, Agent Avant submitted the blood collected from Ronald Allen to the SLED forensic lab for DNA testing. SLED Lieutenant Emily Reinhart informed Lieutenant Bob Carter with Walterboro Police that she would need to see all of the evidence that was at Walterboro to check for items that could be tested for DNA now that they had a possible suspect's DNA profile.

Walterboro investigators conducted an inventory of evidence from the 1978 crime scene; however, some items that were on the 1978 evidence log were not located. Unfortunately, the semen swabs collected from Elaine at her autopsy were among the missing items.

Lieutenant Carter then transported the following available evidence from Walterboro Police to SLED:

Vials labeled blood stain
Swabs from rug in living room

Jeans found on roof of back porch belonging to victim Elaine Fogle
Bra, shirt and shoes collected at autopsy belonging to victim Elaine Fogle
1 pair white panties

Agent Avant contacted SLED analyst John Barron, who performed the chemical analysis on the evidence submitted in 1978, for assistance in locating the items that were unaccounted for. He also inquired about items still at SLED that could be tested for DNA. Analyst Barron informed him that cuttings and swabs of the recent resubmitted evidence from Lieutenant Bob Carver had been reexamined for DNA. Reports reflected that DNA was developed on some items, including the vials of blood and cuttings and swabs from Elaine's clothing.

All profiles found were female and belonged to Elaine. None of the DNA developed belonged to a male; therefore, none belonged to the suspect in question, Ronald Allen.

There was no report of an analysis on the pair of white panties, so Lieutenant Carter contacted Analyst Barron and inquired about his testing of the panties. Analyst Barron informed Lieutenant Carter that he did try to isolate DNA from cuttings from the panties, but there was nothing there, so he did not write a report. Even though there had been advancements in DNA technology during the years, the reexamination of the panties with the updated technology failed to locate any DNA.

Coming into question once again were the semen swabs collected from Elaine at the autopsy that had been transferred to Agent Chad Caldwell. The semen would be of major importance now to provide a full DNA profile of Elaine's murderer and rapist. Agent Avant asked for a thorough search of any documentation pertaining to the semen swabs.

SLED's forensic lab had a very strict log-in protocol for submitting evidence for chemical analysis. An official SLED request for laboratory analysis form had to be completed by the requesting agency with relevant information of the crime. When logging evidence at SLED, the request for analysis form was given a case number and date when received, and it would be stamped with a SLED official stamp of the exact date and time received. Any additional evidence submitted at a later date or time would be logged in under the same case number, but the date and time stamp would, of course, be documented as the date and time when the additional evidence was received. In addition to the log-in documentation form, the information was entered in a log-in ledger book and a card index file that reflected the information from the log-in form.

SLED evidence log-in ledger. *Courtesy of SLED.*

While searching for documentation to possibly assist in locating the semen vials, a log-in sheet for SLED Laboratory Analysis Chemistry Department was located in Elaine's case file. It was dated July 5, 1978, and was signed by SLED agent Chad Caldwell. The form reflected three specimens submitted:

1. A vial—vagina swab
2. B vial—rectal swab
3. C vial—mouth swab
Examination requested was: Type semen for blood type and grouping

Of major concern was that there was no SLED case number on this log-in sheet, and there was no official SLED time stamp reflecting the time the vials were logged in to the SLED chemistry lab. The transfer sheet from Dr. Trefny transferring the vials of semen to SLED agent Chad Caldwell on July 5, 1978, was, however, located in Walterboro's case files.

Agent Avant contacted Agent Caldwell and inquired about the semen swabs after he picked them up from Dr. Trefny. Agent Caldwell told him that he had submitted them to SLED.

At this point, there was no male DNA from the crime scene to work with, so there was nothing that could be compared to Ronald Allen's DNA profile or be entered into the CODIS database.

Agent Avant submitted the boot and shoe collected from Ronald Allen's room to the SLED forensics lab to be compared to the photographs of the bloody pattern on Elaine's abdomen that was believed to be a partial bloody shoe print. Because I was familiar with the case and had worked with the photographs in 1978, SLED called me out of retirement to work with the photographs, again using updated advancements in forensic photography.

Numerous enhancements and high-quality photographic techniques were used to bring out more of the bloody pattern on Elaine's abdomen, but when compared to the outsole designs of Allen's boots and shoes, they were determined to not be a match to the bloody pattern on Elaine's abdomen.

The boot and shoe outsoles were also compared to the photograph of the shoe prints found below the windows at the scene in 1978. The size of the boot and shoe were consistent to the shoe prints in the photograph, but neither outsole designs were a match.

During this time, Lieutenant Jack Watson received an interesting call in reference to Ronald Allen from an employee with Colleton County Regional Center in Walterboro. This employee worked in the physical therapy department.

She told him that as part of her clinical nursing process she was assigned Fran Allen, Ronald's wife, to shadow her for a day. She took Fran around and showed her the procedural process of assisting with physical therapy treatments. They talked afterward, and the subject of Elaine's murder came up.

During the conversation, the employee said that Fran stated to her that her husband, known as "Bear," might have killed Elaine because he had scratches on his face when he came home that morning. Fran told her she didn't want to tell anyone when it happened because she was very scared of Ronald.

When asked if she and Fran were friends, the employee replied, "I knew Fran, but I wasn't what you would call a friend." Lieutenant Watson became somewhat skeptical of the information she had offered, as he was well aware that Ronald Allen had been known around Walterboro as "Hammer" not "Bear." This person provided a written statement, and it was documented and placed in Elaine's case file.

Several months later, after receiving final reports of all of the resubmitted evidence from the SLED forensic lab, investigators decided to present their new findings, including the interviews with Ronald Allen's brothers, to the Colleton County solicitor.

They asked for his consideration that Ronald Allen was the key suspect at the time of the murder in 1978. They discussed the circumstantial evidence—possible trophies, boot and shoe size consistencies, accounts from brothers—along with the fact that Ronald Allen was now deceased, in hopes of closing the case.

The solicitor informed the investigators that because there was no positive evidence linking Ronald Allen to Elaine's murder, he would not move forward with charges against Allen. Elaine's case was put back on the shelf, remaining Walterboro's number one cold case.

While I was working with the photos at SLED, investigators updated me on some details of what had happened with the case over the years. With these updates from the investigators and some of my own personal documentation of the progress and memories on Elaine's case, I decided to set out on my own personal quest to obtain any information that I could.

Maybe, after all the years, it would spark someone's memory to remember something or somebody who might be helpful and of utmost importance and could be passed on to investigators.

13.
SOUTH CAROLINA TRUE CRIME PUBLICATIONS

Twenty-Eight Years after the Murder, 2006

In 2006, my first book, *Carolina Crimes, Case Files of a Forensic Photographer*, was published, followed in 2007 by *Murder in the Midlands, Larry Gene Bell and the 28 Days of Terror in South Carolina*. For my next book, *Small-Town Slayings in South Carolina*, I decided to go back in time with some crimes that I remembered as a child growing up with my family in the rural area around Orangeburg, South Carolina. I wanted to show differences and similarities of crime solving from past and present, bringing in how the suspects were apprehended by good old-fashioned police work and technology before all of this amazing advanced technology became available.

I included a murder and assault I had assisted with that happened in Sumter, South Carolina, in 1989. It was solved fifteen years later, in 2004, through the use of DNA and the killer's bloody fingerprint on the victim's black pocketbook found on her bed. The female victim, twenty-nine-year-old Joyce Robinson, was brutally stabbed, murdered and sexually assaulted. A major development in this case was that test results from the blood collected at the scene revealed two different blood types, proving that there were two bleeders at the scene. It is not unusual for an attacker to injure himself during a violent attack, so this indicated that he was also injured.

The bloody fingerprint on the pocketbook was another crucial piece of evidence. SLED fingerprint examiners determined that the fingerprint was not the victim's. SLED serology analysts determined that the blood in the fingerprint was also not the victim's, which indicated the strong possibility that the fingerprint and the blood belonged to her attacker.

The events in this case were similar to Elaine's, as there was a large amount of blood, semen and fingerprints collected from the crime scene, but there were no suspects to compare this evidence to.

In 1989, because there was no AFIS database, the fingerprints could be compared to the known prints of a suspect to check for a possible match. DNA technology could provide a DNA profile from blood and semen. A profile was developed on a bloody towel in the bathroom. The DNA database CODIS was also not available, so to test for a possible match, a known DNA sample would have to be collected from a potential suspect to compare to the DNA evidence from the crime scene.

As with Elaine's case, investigators could not let go of this one. They knew they had fingerprints and blood from the crime scene that did not belong to the victim, but they had no suspects. Years passed, and with no arrests, Joyce's murder and sexual assault became a cold case.

In the mid-90s, the DNA CODIS database set-up had begun. With each day and each new entry, the DNA database continued to grow. SLED serologist Ira Jeffcoat always knew they had a good DNA profile of the attacker, and fingerprints left at the crime scene were on file in the SLED photography and latent print lab.

In 2004, fifteen years after the murder, Jeffcoat had all the evidence from the 1989 crime scene on file at the Sumter Police Department resubmitted to the SLED forensics lab for reexamination. Working with some newly advanced DNA technology, SLED analyst David McClure developed an updated DNA profile from the blood on the towel. The profile was entered in the CODIS database.

A match was returned from CODIS belonging to an Earl Mack, but it was not an exact DNA match to the profile from the bloody towel. This eliminated Earl Mack but indicated that he was a close male relative of the person whose DNA was collected from the bloody towel. Updated DNA technology now had the potential of recognizing relatives to a certain degree of a known DNA profile if it was in CODIS. A previous arrest of Earl Mack had resulted in his DNA being entered into the CODIS database.

Examiners now needed to locate all immediate male family members of Earl Mack. A SLED records search revealed that there were three male members of Earl Mack's family who had arrest records and fingerprint cards on file at SLED. Lieutenant Tom Darnell, SLED latent print examiner, performed fingerprint comparisons on all three of the individuals with the photograph of the bloody fingerprint on the pocketbook.

Lieutenant Darnell positively identified the bloody fingerprint to the left index finger of Tony Mack, Earl Mack's brother. This placed Tony Mack at the crime scene, and it gave investigators a name to work with.

Lieutenant Darnell was known to always go that extra mile with all of his cases. Although he had made a positive match to the photograph of the fingerprint on the pocketbook, he had the pocketbook resubmitted to the SLED fingerprint lab and conducted a visual examination of the fingerprint on the pocketbook. Again, he confirmed a positive match of the fingerprint on the pocketbook to Tony Mack. He also performed latent print comparisons of prints lifted from around the bathroom sink in the home. They were also positive matches to Tony Mack.

Sumter Police investigators located Tony Mack in Fayetteville, North Carolina. Mack said he did know Joyce but he did not kill her and voluntarily gave a blood sample. His blood was submitted to the SLED DNA lab for testing. Tony Mack's DNA profile was an exact match to the DNA profile from the bloody towel in the bathroom sink and from the bloody fingerprint on the pocketbook. DNA of additional evidence from the scene were also positive matches to Tony Mack.

The overwhelming forensic evidence in this case could not be disputed. Tony Mack left behind many clues and his personal signatures. The evidence was there all along. What changed was the way it was examined with new technology. Tony Mack accepted a plea deal and was sentenced to thirty years.

I was hopeful that including this case in my book might bring attention to how a cold case could be solved after many years with determined investigators staying on the case and never giving up. That's when I decided that the final chapter in my third book would be "The Unsolved Murder of Gwendolyn Elaine Fogle." It was my hope that documenting Elaine's case by putting it down in writing might bring it back to the public's eyes and, of most importance, to investigator's eyes.

14

Meeting Elaine Fogle's Family

Twenty-Nine Years after the Murder, June 2007

I had never met any of Elaine Fogle's family over all the years that her case had been in my life. But in June 2007, with the help of my longtime friend and partner at SLED Captain David Caldwell, we located Elaine's sister, Eolean, in Clinton, South Carolina.

I sent a letter to Eolean, introduced myself and told her how I had been involved with her sister's case since 1978. I told her how much it had touched me personally and remained with me through the years. I shared my thoughts of including Elaine's case in my upcoming book and said that I would like to meet with her and her family members if they were interested in assisting me with any information, personal or otherwise, that they might want me to include.

Because the case was still unsolved, I informed her that I would be limited in what I could include involving the progress of the investigation, as most of that was never released to the public, but anything that had been made public by media coverage could be included.

Several weeks passed, and I didn't get a reply. Of course, I thought that it might be too painful for her to revisit all of this or, even worse, that she had passed away. I kept hope, and in late July 2007, I received the following letter from Eolean:

Lt. Rita Y. Shuler (retired)
Dear Ms. Shuler,

I was very thrilled and humbled when I received your letter, with your gracious offer to write about my sister Elaine and her murder, and I am so sorry that it has taken so long to respond to it.

I have had several health problems recently, but I am doing better now.

Thank you so much for your interest in Elaine's case.

When I spoke to my family members they were glad to know that someone else cared about our loved one. They have responded and are in favor of whatever you could do to find the one who did this terrible deed.

My mother and father and I tried to do all we could when and after it happened, but the lack of money to pursue it was a problem. They have been deceased for many years, and I still do not have any means to follow it up, so I am glad that you would want to do this for us.

Since I am the only one left in my immediate family, my aunts and cousins will help in remembering her and how she died.

My aunt, Winnie Brickle has encouraged me to write down all that I can remember, and she will do the same. Since she and her family were out of state when it occurred, they do not have a lot of memories of the immediate crime scene.

I will try to remember all that I can and write them down so that you can use what you can to write about Elaine's case.

I will try to get this to you as soon as possible.

Thank you so much for caring to do this. You will never know how much this has helped my aunts and me. We were at the point that we thought nobody cared and Elaine had been forgotten.

It's nice to know that there are still people who care about others.

God bless you for this.

Sincerely,
Eolean Fogle Hughes

I was touched by Eolean's reply, and we made plans to meet. This was when Elaine's family entered my life, and it was the beginning of an amazing closeness and caring friendship.

On my first visit with Eolean, as she met me at the door, she had a surprised look on her face, and at first, I wasn't sure what to make of it. Then she smiled and said, "Oh my goodness, you look like Elaine. Y'all could be sisters." After I caught my breath, this just strengthened my feelings of the connection to Elaine.

Her next statement took my breath again: "The way my family has been treated over the years, we thought Elaine had been forgotten. Thank you for caring." I assured her that maybe she was forgotten by some, but not by everyone.

It didn't take me long to realize that this was one tough lady. I could feel Elaine's spirit and strength in her, thinking back to how Elaine had fought to save her life. Eolean had a memory like an elephant and the heart of an angel.

Conversation came easy. I just let her talk, and this lady did talk:

> *Elaine was my best friend. She was a tomboy growing up. She loved to ride her bike all over Orangeburg. We would go to Edisto Gardens all the time. She was in a lot of church clubs at our church, the Palmetto Street Church of God. She loved children. She worked at a nursery with our mom until she graduated from the Orangeburg Regional Technical School in 1972. She loved doing all kinds of things with our mom and dad, grandmama, aunts, uncles, and cousins. Elaine loved to draw and paint and started taking art courses. She painted pictures and gave them to her family the Christmas before she was killed. We were all very close. She was always kind to people. When somebody didn't have a place to stay, she would open up her home to them. Elaine had gotten engaged before she was killed. Her fiancé stayed in touch with our family for a while after her death.*

Eolean's following statement was chilling. "One thing that Elaine used to do still bothers me every time I think about it. Elaine loved life so much and was so comfortable where she was in life. She would strut around the house and laugh saying, 'When I die, I'm gonna make history.' I guess in a way she did, but not the way any of us would have ever imagined."

Eolean told me, "I watch *Forensic Files* and *Cold Case Files* faithfully on TV, and I see how old cases are being solved with all the new technology. I've prayed that this will be the answer to solving Elaine's murder, but I was told years ago that her case was closed." I assured her that Elaine's case was not closed. Yes, it was a cold case, but a cold case is never closed; it's just sleeping, waiting on new leads and investigators to finally dig out the truth.

I was in overload with her memories and details when I left, but this was good. Eolean's information filled in some blanks for me, learning how hard she and her family had struggled to get justice for her sister.

Elaine (*left*) and her sister Eolean. *Courtesy of Eolean Fogle Hughes.*

On my next visit with Eolean and Larry, as I walked inside, she pointed to my picture she had placed next to Elaine's picture on her living room mantel. She told me, "You and Elaine would have been very good friends. You know, you're family now."

Left: Mr. and Mrs. Fogle, Elaine *(front left)* and sister Eolean at Easter service. *Courtesy of Eolean Fogle Hughes.*

Right: Elaine loved riding her bike around town. *Courtesy of Eolean Fogle Hughes.*

I soon realized how serious she was about that. On every holiday and birthday, I received a card from Eolean and Larry. She invited me to their family reunions, which were held at Antley's Bar-B-Q restaurant in Orangeburg, South Carolina. There I met and talked to her extended family and got my fill of that delicious country barbecue. I would also get invitations to visit them on their annual summer beach trips to Sullivan's Island, South Carolina.

Some family members informed me that they had attempted to communicate with Walterboro Police Department through the years, hoping to keep the investigation ongoing, and were always told that there was nothing new.

Continuing my research of Elaine's case for my book, I decided to try my luck and write a few letters to people who were key players during the initial investigation. Lieutenant Bob Carter with Walterboro Police Department, the lead investigator on Elaine's case since day one, responded and agreed to meet with me. Talking to him, I could feel that this case was his baby from the very beginning, and he wanted it solved. He shared information that he could without jeopardizing the still ongoing investigation.

Sometimes you just have to read between the lines, and I did just that. I came up with some thoughts of my own. I connected with Nancy Hooker,

Shuler (*right*) and Elaine's sister, Eolean, at family reunion. *Author's collection.*

Elaine's roommate, and friend Billy O'Bryant. Nancy had moved out of state. Billy still lived in Walterboro. They refreshed me on the early morning when they entered the house and found Elaine's body. I could still feel their pain as they told me the details, as well as their compassion for Elaine. They were so thankful to find out that someone was still trying to find the person who murdered their friend.

I contacted assistant solicitor Steve Knight of the Fourteenth Circuit in Colleton County. I had assisted Solicitor Knight with some cases during my tenure with SLED and also knew him on a personal level through friends. After informing him of my connection with this case over the years, I asked for his guidance in moving forward with a new investigation.

Solicitor Knight remembered Elaine's murder and informed me that he would have his investigator Charles Griffith check on the status of the case at Walterboro Police Department. Investigator Griffith met with Major Ken Dasen and found that there was still a room full of evidence on file in the department.

Solicitor Knight was very positive after learning about all of the evidence that had been preserved through the years and strongly believed the case should be looked into again. He told me, "Whatever you have to do to get

SLED involved in this again, do it!" He had Griffith provide me copies of some files that needed to be presented to SLED.

Another one of my contacts was Dr. Frank Trefny, who responded to the crime scene in 1978, photographed the scene and performed Elaine's autopsy. He was now in private practice in Kingstree, South Carolina. He was very gracious and shared with me how he never forgot Elaine's case and offered what he could remember from his involvement in 1978. We talked about how DNA might be the key to solving the case now.

He distinctly remembered how carefully he had collected the semen from Elaine's body and preserved it in appropriate vials. He remembered meeting with SLED agent Chad Caldwell and transferring the vials of semen to him to be submitted to the SLED chemistry lab for further testing.

I asked about any photographs of the crime scene or autopsy that he might still have. As best as he could remember, he had left them with the Walterboro Police Department or with the Colleton Regional Hospital, where the autopsy was performed.

Lieutenant Carter had informed me during my meeting with him that the autopsy photographs were not in Walterboro's files, so I went to the Colleton Regional Hospital and asked about any records it might have on Elaine's case. The employees, too, were very gracious and checked their files. Unfortunately, they had no information relating to Elaine Fogle. They did acknowledge that some files were destroyed during Hurricane Hugo's devastation to the Walterboro area in September 1989.

Included in the documents I received from the solicitor's office were two transfer sheets dated May 30, 1978, reflecting right- and left-hand fingernail scrapings collected from Elaine at the autopsy. A chain of custody showed that Dr. Trefny had transferred the fingernail scrapings to Lieutenant Bob Carter at the Walterboro Police Department. On that same day, Lieutenant Carter delivered and transferred the fingernail scrapings to Dr. Sandra Conradi, forensic pathologist with the Medical University of South Carolina (MUSC), for her expert analysis. A document from the medical university, dated March 28, 1984, reflected that the vials of fingernail scrapings were released to SLED agent Chad Caldwell. Agent Caldwell then transferred the vials of fingernail scrapings back to Lieutenant Bob Carter. No official analysis report from the medical university were located in the files.

Dr. Conradi performed autopsies for many SLED investigations. I was present at some of them, so I knew her on a professional level during my years with SLED. I also knew Sandra on a personal level, as we were both avid runners. We ran in some of the same road races over the years and shared some interesting experiences. On one occasion, after finishing a road race in Charleston, she got called to MUSC to perform an autopsy and invited me to go along. There we were in the autopsy room in our running attire as she proceeded with the process. It was quite a memorable experience.

We were both retired now, so I contacted her to ask for direction to locate any files on Elaine's case that might still be at MUSC, since she had received the fingernail scrapings in 1978. She did remember the Fogle case, but because the autopsy was not performed at MUSC, she advised that there might be no specimens retained at MUSC. She also had a concern that Hurricane Hugo's devastation to Charleston wiped out many files.

Dr. Conradi suggested having an investigator or Solicitor Knight issue a subpoena to MUSC Forensic Pathology Department to check on any specimens, medical documents and files pertaining to Elaine Fogle. I contacted Solicitor Steve Knight, and he sent a subpoena to administrative assistant Maxine Robinson at the MUSC lab. Unfortunately, no specimens, medical documents or files were found.

I then turned my attention back to SLED and contacted the director of SLED at that time, Reginald Lloyd. I included information on Elaine's case, along with some progress notes of the investigation in the recent years and asked if he would consider meeting with me and possibly assign a SLED investigator to the case. I got no response.

In a personal conversation with several SLED investigators who I had previously worked with, I inquired about the possibility of volunteering to assist with looking over Elaine's case with them. They were very receptive of my offer, but it never progressed any further.

I continued to stay in close contact with Elaine's family. Elaine's uncle James Fogle had become involved in assisting Eolean with gathering any helpful information and communicating with Walterboro Police Department to keep up with the status of Elaine's case. He had struggled through the years after losing Elaine, and he became determined to do all he could to find the person who had murdered her and brought so much grief and heartache to his family.

Once again, months and years passed with no developments.

15.

SLED OPENS COLD CASE UNIT

Thirty-One Years after the Murder, 2009

In 2009, my third book, *Small-Town Slayings in South Carolina*, was published. "The Unsolved Murder of Gwendolyn Elaine Fogle" was the final chapter. So many questions remained unanswered, but somebody out there knew what happened, and I thought getting the story out to the public again might jog someone's memory or work on their conscience to finally come forward and tell the truth.

In February 2009, writer George Salsberry did a full-page cover story in the *Press and Standard* on Elaine's story being a part of my book. The headline read, "Still Looking for a Killer, Search for Killer Never Ends." This brought Elaine's murder back to the forefront for residents. In March 2009, Downtown Books and Espresso in Walterboro invited me for a book signing event.

It was heartening to meet and have residents share their Elaine stories with me, while also feeling their sadness of losing her and still being afraid that her murderer was still out there. They were very hopeful that this would open new eyes to the investigation. One touching moment for me was when I heard a familiar voice say, "Hey, Ms. Rita, remember me?" It was Billy O'Bryant, Elaine's friend who had found her that fatal night. Billy had graciously talked to me when I was gathering information on my own and shared his pain of never getting over that night, so we shared a closeness.

Some residents who had moved away from Walterboro over the years still subscribed to the *Press and Standard* newspaper and read about the renewed interest and coverage of Elaine's murder.

In March 2009, Tucker Lyon, writer with the *Times and Democrat* newspaper of Elaine's hometown of Orangeburg, included a full-page editorial titled "Ripped from the Headlines." She detailed the true crime stories connected to the Orangeburg area that I had chronicled—one in 1955 in Orangeburg, one in 1974 from neighboring Calhoun County and Elaine's case in 1978.

So, as Elaine's story became widespread again, the Walterboro Police investigators began receiving some interesting feedback and tips, but the information led nowhere.

Then one day as I was looking around on Facebook, I saw that SLED had set up a cold case unit. On the unit's page, it read, "Thank you for visiting the South Carolina Law Enforcement Division's Cold Case Unit. The following are cases that SLED is working in conjunction with local law enforcement. If you have any information, please click onto the following link to leave your information. You do not have to leave your name but if you want an agent to call you, please provide your contact information." Elaine Fogle's murder was the first on the list, so I jumped on it and called SLED's cold case unit.

A meeting was set with Agents Bo Barton and Natalie Crosland, both of whom I had worked with while at SLED. I advised them of my history working on this case over the years and my contact with Deputy Solicitor Knight, informing that there was still a room full of evidence at the Walterboro Police Department. I provided them with all of the documents he had sent to me and shared information that I had gathered while doing research for my book. I informed them about the missing semen swabs from Elaine's autopsy that had never been located over the years. They agreed that the swabs would be extremely beneficial for obtaining a DNA profile of the killer.

The news that SLED had formed a cold case unit once again brought new hope to Elaine's case. Walterboro reporter Geroge Salsberry of the *Press and Standard* included an editorial in the August 3, 2010 edition: "DNA from 32-year-old murder case being processed by SLED." He wrote of SLED's newly organized unit that would assist local law enforcement agencies in their efforts to solve long-forgotten violent crimes through the use of new advanced technology. He included that SLED's website offered a brief description of Elaine Fogle's murder on May 27, 1978, which had rocked

The Press and Standard
Tuesday, August 3, 2010

Crime

■ COLD CASE

DNA from 32-year-old murder case being processed by SLED

Fogle murder is oldest unsolved case on SLED's website.

ELAINE FOGLE

Courtesy of the Press and Standard.

Walterboro for over three decades. It was the oldest cold case listed on SLED's website.

Major Ken Dasen of the Walterboro Police Department stated in the article that those who originally investigated the murder had a suspect in the case but were never able to link him to the murder. He said that the suspect later moved out of the state and was now deceased, but his death would not deter the effort to close the case. Dasen continued, stating that in late 2009, two members of SLED's cold case unit came to Walterboro Police Department and collected the evidence from the Fogle murder. It was resubmitted to the SLED forensic lab for testing, and the DNA of the deceased suspect was now on file at SLED. Dasen concluded by saying that investigators hoped that advancements in DNA would one day reach the point that they could link the deceased suspect and victim and clear the case.

Mr. Salsberry also included an interview he had conducted with me the year before, including my statement that this case has remained with me since the beginning in 1978.

I remained anxious to know of any progress on the case, and at times, I had to just sit back and take a deep breath and do whatever it took to get through the moment. Usually, I would go out for a run and get in touch with my thoughts and nature.

One day as I was having one of those moments, I had just gotten out of the house and went to the grocery store. While going through the check-out line, I had a chance encounter with SLED cold case agent Natalie

Crosland. After hellos, she informed me, "I have really become involved in Elaine's case and have met with Walterboro Police Department, collected some of the evidence they had and resubmitted it to SLED forensic department for reexamination."

She shared with me how this case had touched her deeply as well and that she understood my passion for it through all these years. I knew she could not tell me any investigative details, but she did say, "I think we have some new results from the original evidence that could possibly help solve this case."

This just raised my curiosity to another level. My first thought was that maybe, just maybe, they located the semen swabs from the autopsy, which might now provide a DNA profile of the suspect. Though I didn't know any pertinent details, just knowing that Agent Crosland was diligently working on it was music to my ears.

I informed Elaine's sister of SLED's cold case unit, my meeting with them and the information that they had given me. I told her about the conversation I had with Agent Crosland in the grocery store and that it sounded positive.

After some time passed, I received a call from Agent Crosland informing me that SLED's cold case unit had been disbanded, and she was being transferred to the vehicle crimes unit. Again, she told me how Elaine's case had become very important to her, and she really wanted to do more. She asked if there was any way I might contact SLED to try to keep the investigation ongoing and inquire about the possibility of me assisting.

I followed Agent Crosland's suggestions and wrote letters, sent emails and made calls to SLED and Walterboro Police Department. I received no response.

I hated to have to give Elaine's sister the news that SLED's cold case unit had been disbanded, but at the same time, I told her to never give up hope, as we had faced many ups and downs before. Eolean let me know that she and Larry had some medical issues and needed some help at times, and through friends, they had met a lady who was willing to assist them. That's when Melissa Hughes entered their lives. She became very involved with their everyday care and helped in keeping up with the progress of Elaine's investigation.

When Eolean introduced me to Melissa as her adopted daughter, I knew exactly where she was coming from. I certainly knew how much family meant to her. I just smiled and said, "Well, I guess we're all family now."

Around this same time, Elaine's cousin James contacted me and said that he was still doing some investigating on his own. He had contacted SLED and Walterboro Police Department through the years, but he had received very little response. He was adamant that he would definitely continue to pursue any information and communicate with Walterboro Police Department and SLED.

Then, again, it seemed like time just stopped. Months and years came and went. It is sad but true: cold cases aren't the priority of law enforcement agencies; today's murders are.

16

NEW EYES, NEW INVESTIGATORS

Thirty-Seven Years after the Murder, May 27, 2015

Realizing another dream of mine in 2013, I relocated to South Carolina's beautiful coast in the charming Lowcountry area of Johns Island. I was living my dream of being an island girl, loving the sunshine, the beach and the laid-back, easy, good life. I was beaching, crabbing, fishing and shark tooth hunting as much as I could.

My passion for forensics and investigations remained as strong as ever, and I continued to research and keep abreast of forensics and new technology as it was continuously evolving. I forever watched *Forensic Files*, the Investigative ID Channel and documentaries of true crime programs. I will admit that one of my guilty pleasures is *Law and Order: Special Victims Unit*. I have probably watched every episode that has aired. Even though *SVU* isn't true crime, it is very watchable and covers some strong ripped-from-the-headlines stories.

My retirement and relocation to the coast took me farther from Elaine's family, but the personal closeness continued. Elaine was always in our conversations. Eolean told me that every year on the anniversary of Elaine's death, she would read Elaine's story in my book, and every time, she could feel Elaine's presence there saying, "Don't give up on me, Sis."

On May 27, 2015, the thirty-seventh anniversary of Elaine's death, Eolean and Melissa called me. They said after reading the story, they had a strong feeling that it was time to call Walterboro Police Department again and hear what they had to say about the investigation now. And that's what they did.

In a matter of minutes, Melissa called me back and says, "Ms. Rita you better sit down, 'cause you ain't gonna believe this!" She had spoken to the administrative assistant at Walterboro Police Department and was told that they had a new investigator, Corporal Gean Johnson, already reviewing Elaine's case.

Melissa was immediately put through to Corporal Johnson. He told her that the former police chief was no longer with the Walterboro Police Department, and when he came on board, the new police chief, Wade Marvin, approached him with the history of Elaine's unsolved case. Chief Marvin had given him a folder full of documentation of communication from members of the Fogle family inquiring about updates and progress on her case over the years. Corporal Johnson told Melissa, "Elaine's case is one that I have started looking into to solve."

Shocked but totally overjoyed, Eolean and Melissa then advised Corporal Johnson that I had been helping them through the years with Elaine's case and to please consider talking to me and having me assist him with the new investigation. I was very excited about their news, and just a few minutes later, I received a call from Corporal Johnson.

He told me that one of his wife's coworkers had attended my book signing in Walterboro in March 2009 and had my book *Small-Town Slayings in South Carolina*. Her coworker gave her a copy of Elaine's story to pass on to him, saying, "Now that he is an investigator with the Walterboro Police Department, maybe he can solve it, because no one could in the past."

Corporal Johnson graciously said to me, "I started reading the story, and I was even more encouraged, when I saw that you had worked with SLED and you have been involved with Elaine's case from the very beginning and followed it all through the years."

He asked me to assist him with his new investigation. I couldn't say yes fast enough. It was definitely an over the moon and a divine hand to God moment for me. I informed him that I was not an active law enforcement officer since my retirement, and I would need authorization from Police Chief Marvin to assist him so that I would be allowed to have full access to all files and evidence.

He had already talked to Chief Marvin, who had given his wholehearted and official approval for me to assist as a retired agent with SLED. I assured Chief Marvin that my assistance would be in a voluntary consulting capacity, with no monetary requests. I had all the time in the world for Elaine and her family. I had been trying for so many years, hoping that one day I would be allowed to join investigators and offer my assistance. Now, it had happened. I would be assisting this dedicated and passionate investigator, and I would finally be allowed access to all of the files and evidence.

The timing was good, as well. My drive from Johns Island to Walterboro would be easy. I could assist with the investigation at the Walterboro Police Department and work from my home. Thus it began again. Elaine Fogle's murder investigation was finally—after almost four decades—off the shelf and back on the forefront.

Corporal Gean Johnson started at the Walterboro Police Department with fourteen years of experience in investigations and twenty-three years of experience as a police officer. He grew up in the small quiet country town of Smoaks, South Carolina. Smoaks is twenty miles from Walterboro and had a population of about 125.

He began his childhood dream of being in law enforcement in February 1992, working with the Colleton County Sheriff's Office in Walterboro as a detention officer in the capacity of a shift sergeant.

In May 1994, he graduated from the eight-week basic police training program at the South Carolina Criminal Justice Academy in Columbia, South Carolina, and moved on to the patrol division at the Colleton County Sheriff's Office, working his way up to the rank of sergeant. He worked patrol for approximately seven years and then transferred to criminal investigations.

After several years as sergeant of the Criminal Investigations Unit, he was then promoted to lieutenant, before becoming the captain in charge of the criminal investigation division. This promotion put him in charge of other divisions that also came under his chain of command.

Along the way, he received advanced training in law enforcement specialty areas, such as interview and interrogation, crime scene investigation, death investigation and fingerprint identification, as well as attending many law enforcement seminars. While moving up in the ranks, he attended management training programs, several of which were executive level.

After twenty-two years with the Colleton County Sheriff's Office, in April 2014, he made another change. He went to work for the Dorchester County Sheriff's Office in Summerville, South Carolina, working mostly in civil and family court proceedings as a court security officer. After about a year of learning much about court procedures, he also learned that he wasn't ready to settle on that just yet, because in his heart, he knew how much he really "missed the mysteries of investigating things."

Following his heart, in February 2015, he returned to Colleton County and started working at the Walterboro Police Department as a criminal investigator.

My first formal meeting with Corporal Johnson was June 3, 2015, at the Walterboro Police Department. Within minutes of meeting him, I felt like I had known this man forever. He looked like a big ol' muscular teddy bear, and he had a gentleness and passion about him that just makes a heart feel good.

Corporal Johnson admitted that when he saw the room full of files and boxes on the case, his first thought was, "Wow, do I really want to take this on? I was only thirteen years old in 1978 when it happened." This was the first time I heard him say, "Wow," but it was far from the last. It came up during the course of our weeks and months of the investigation ahead. When I heard him say, "Wow," I knew we were on to something.

He shared with me, "When I opened the first box and starting reviewing it, that was all it took. I ended up carrying some of the files home, and that's something I have never done before in my entire career in law

Corporal Gean Johnson and retired SLED agent lieutenant Rita Shuler. *Photo by Vicky Hall.*

enforcement. I knew this would be the biggest challenge in my twenty-two years of law enforcement, but I was gonna give it my best. Elaine's family has waited long enough to find out who killed her. I have prayed to God to help me solve this case."

I also had the privilege of meeting Police Chief Wade Marvin. He was a lifelong resident of Colleton County and was familiar with Elaine's horrific homicide in 1978. He was so very gracious, thanking us for our assistance in moving forward with the investigation and offering unlimited help from his department.

There was a lot of information that I had not been privy to since my retirement from law enforcement, but now, with official authorization from Chief Marvin, I had all of the files and evidence available. Walterboro officer Amye Stivender, evidence custodian, had re-inventoried and listed every piece of evidence that was still in Elaine's file, but it was not in any particular order.

Corporal Johnson and I laid out everything, put our heads together and went to work organizing the files in a timeline. We started by going back to the very beginning, from the first incident report, dated May 27, 1978, and worked our way to the present, getting an overview of what had happened with the investigation over the years. We went through report after report after report and statement after statement after statement.

One of the first documents we read was the pathologist's autopsy report, and we found the documentation of semen collected from Elaine's body. We knew how important any DNA would be now because of the CODIS database, so a main focus would be any documentation of the semen swabs from 1978 or any evidence from the crime scene that might offer DNA. A DNA profile from the semen entered into CODIS could possibly be a positive link to Elaine's killer.

On my ride home that first day, Corporal Johnson's words kept playing over and over in my mind: "I have to solve this for Elaine and her family." So many times over the years, Elaine's case was pulled off the shelf and then put back, unsolved. After meeting with Corporal Johnson, I could feel his passion and knew that this time would be different. This seasoned investigator and caring man would not put it back on the shelf unsolved.

Days and evenings ahead were spent reviewing and evaluating reports, crime scene photographs and evidence. Corporal Johnson and I came up with new questions and theories, and we both would have to admit that some of the theories might have sounded a little bizarre, but we went with them, as they might prove helpful.

Lieutenant Craig Stivender with the Walterboro Police Department had, at times, consulted with Beaufort County Sheriff's Department in Beaufort, South Carolina, for assistance on several of Walterboro's existing cases. Corporal Johnson and Lieutenant Stivender met with Captain Bob Bromage with Beaufort County and discussed Elaine's case with him. They also inquired about the possibility of Beaufort's DNA lab assisting with re-examining some of the evidence.

As I continued to review Elaine's files, I observed a copy of an email from Captain Bromage to Lieutenant Stivender that was a recap of their meeting. Captain Bromage noted that there was interesting evidence with potential. He advised to do a check on the origin of the panties with the DNA mixture to establish how the panties are related to the incident.

When I read this, I asked Corporal Johnson, "What is this mixed DNA Captain Bromage is referring to?" Corporal Johnson pointed out that a SLED report from 2010 reflected that mixed DNA was found on a pair of panties from the crime scene. I read the SLED report and saw that it was signed by SLED agent Natalie Crosland.

I gasped, "Oh my God, this is SLED cold case agent Natalie Crosland's report from back in 2010. This is what she was trying to get across to me when we saw each other in the grocery store, but she couldn't tell me the details."

Knowing that mixed DNA is a mixture from more than one individual, we reviewed the SLED report and saw that a combination of female and male DNA had been found on the panties. Agent Crosland's notes reflected that in 2009, while in SLED's cold case unit, she collected some evidence from Walterboro to be resubmitted for review and analysis. These panties from the crime scene were among the evidence that was resubmitted.

She submitted the panties to the SLED DNA department for analysis. Blood was detected. A mixed DNA profile was developed from the blood on the panties by DNA analyst Laura Mills. There was a male contributor and a female contributor.

The female profile was identified as Elaine Fogle's. The male profile was unknown. This was certainly another hand to God moment. At least now we knew that there was some male DNA from the crime scene to work with. This would show that at some point blood belonging to the person who attacked Elaine came into contact with her blood, forming the combined mixture of her blood and his blood, and it was transferred to the panties. We thought that he had possibly cut himself when breaking the window to enter the house or possibly during the struggle when Elaine was fighting back.

The report also reflected that Agent Crosland had Analyst Mills, do a comparison of the male DNA profile found on the panties to the longtime suspect, Ronald Allen, whose DNA profile was now on file at SLED. Mills's summary result of that comparison stated, "The partial DNA profile developed from item 26.1 (cuttings from panties) is a mixture of at least two individuals, one male and one female. The partial DNA profile developed from the male contributor to this mixture has been entered into the Combined DNA Index System (CODIS). Ronald Allen is excluded as a possible contributor in this mixture."

Crosland included in her notes that even though Elaine Fogle's DNA was in the mixture, she would need to verify the panties, since it was not clearly documented where the panties were located at the crime scene. Did they belong to the victim or the roommate?

She also noted that the evidence and reports had been returned from SLED to Walterboro Police Department with partial documentation because the solicitor's office or submitting agency had declared this case was closed or DNA analysis was not needed at the time. This meant that although SLED now had unknown male DNA in the case, it could not move forward to check for a match until there was a known DNA sample from a suspect to check against the unknown DNA profile developed from the panties. She also noted that, with the unknown male DNA profile now in CODIS, there was a possibility that a match could be returned at any time.

We found that all of the evidence that the SLED cold case unit had resubmitted for new analysis in 2009 had been returned from SLED to the Walterboro Police Department in October 2014. The panties in question were one of the items of evidence that were returned from SLED. It was of utmost importance now that we find the panties and determine their location in the crime scene.

We did another search through the case files and found no documentation that Elaine's case had any new progress since SLED's cold case unit reviewed it and reported the new findings to Walterboro in 2010.

A bag containing one pair of white panties was located among the evidence, with documentation that they had been submitted to SLED in 1978. Referring back to the SLED lab report from 1978, results of examination of the panties showed that only pubic hair belonging to the victim was found on the panties at that time, and the panties were then returned to the Walterboro Police Department.

Other documentation showed that the same white panties were resubmitted to SLED in 2001, when the case was evaluated again, but no

DNA was found, and the panties were again returned to the Walterboro Police Department. There was also documentation on the bag containing the pair of white panties reflecting that they had been resubmitted to SLED in 2009 and returned from SLED to Walterboro Police Department in October 2014.

Another bag was found with two pairs of bikini-style panties with colored patterns. Noted on the bag, "From roommate's bedroom." There was no documentation showing that the bikini panties were resubmitted to SLED in 2009. This verified that these were not the panties from which the mixed DNA profile was developed because they had never been submitted to SLED in 2009.

Another verification of the panties was a review of SLED behavioral profiler captain David Caldwell's report of the crime scene in 1989. He had noted that a pair of "old lady" type panties were on the couch in the living room where Elaine's body was found.

We then went back and reviewed the crime scene photos. There were several views that showed the pair of white panties on the couch in the living room where Elaine's body was found. A walking cane was laying on top of them.

Going one step further, I called Elaine's former roommate, Nancy Hooker, and briefed her on the new investigation of Elaine's murder. She wanted to help. I came right out and asked her what type of panties she wore back then, "bikini" or "old lady."

She answered, "Oh, my goodness, I have never worn old lady panties. I always wore bikini panties."

I spoke to Elaine's sister and asked her if she knew what type of panties she had worn. She replies, "She wore the old lady type panties. She didn't like the bikini ones." This information was enough to confirm that the panties

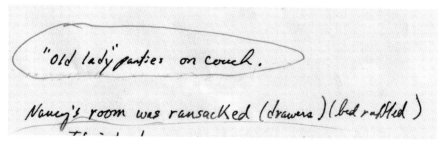

Captain David Caldwell, SLED profiler note. *Elaine Fogle case file.*

Mixed DNA profile was developed from panties on couch in room of attack. *Elaine Fogle case file.*

in question in the report in 2010 were the old lady type that were located on the couch in the living room, and they belonged to the victim. Verifying the panties was a big step forward, but we still did not have a suspect to compare to the male contributor of the DNA.

Another thought we pondered was that the violence and brutality of Elaine's assault could fit the profile of a crime of passion murder. This brought focus again to any boyfriends or close male acquaintances Elaine may have had. Nancy Hooker and Billy O'Bryant both said they did not remember Elaine dating anyone around the time of her death, but she had been engaged at one time. Neither remembered her former fiancé's name.

Elaine's sister and Melissa provided us with the engagement announcement from the *Press and Standard*, which gave us the name of her fiancé. An eerie observation we had was that the announcement was in the May 27, 1976 edition of the *Press and Standard*. That was exactly two years to the day before Elaine was murdered.

Corporal Johnson recognized her fiancé's name. He still lived and had a business in Walterboro. Corporal Johnson spoke to him about his and Elaine's relationship. He said that he and Elaine were engaged but broke up about a year before she was murdered. He could not think of anyone who would want to harm her. When asked if he would submit a buccal (cheek) swab for DNA purposes, he was reluctant, saying, "I was in her house a lot, and we were together, so my DNA and fingerprints would probably be there."

He did not submit to giving the buccal swab at that time but advised Corporal Johnson that he would have his attorney contact him. Corporal Johnson informed his attorney that we only needed his swab for DNA purposes of eliminating him as a suspect because he had once dated and was engaged to Elaine. Her ex-fiancé then voluntarily submitted a buccal swab.

Corporal Johnson continued to check all tips and information that came in and obtained buccal swabs from more male persons of interest. He also reviewed the reports on file of the inmates who talked to officers in 1984. Even though they seemed to know some details, one comment stood out to him. They said they snuck into Elaine's house and waited in her closet for her to get home and then attacked her. That did not hold true to all of the evidence that showed the point of entry to be the broken window in the kitchen, and the initial impact to Elaine was near the front door. After doing another check of the inmates involved and the biological evidence we now had, there was nothing that substantially confirmed they had any involvement.

Corporal Johnson came to the same conclusion as original investigators: they probably overheard idle talk about Elaine's murder, as it was all over the street, and they were also looking for a reduced sentence.

An interesting find while going through some old boxes were some dispatcher tapes dated around the days surrounding Elaine's murder. We thought they might contain incoming calls to the Walterboro Police Department that could be helpful. There was no playback machine available at our disposal to play the thirty-seven-year-old tapes, so we did some research, hoping that a recording studio or TV station might have one that would work with the tapes. We contacted a few, but unfortunately, their up-to-date equipment would not accommodate the size of the dispatcher tapes. Researching further, we found some old-time collectors of audiovisual equipment, but again, their equipment would not accommodate the reels.

Our hopes were heightened after speaking with someone at ETV in Columbia. He was willing to help and informed us that he might have some updated equipment for copying the dispatcher tapes to digital audio.

Corporal Johnson and I transported the tapes to the ETV studio, but this equipment also would not accommodate the size of the reels. We met some very caring folks during our research, and it was refreshing to know that even strangers to the case wanted to offer their time and expertise.

Around this time, the *Press and Standard* ran an article titled "New Eyes, Old Murders." It included information on Elaine Fogle's unsolved murder and that it was now being investigated by new eyes and new investigators. It reflected that over the years Fogle's relatives routinely contacted the police department, pleading for another look at the evidence that had been collected. The article also included that my book *Small-Town Slayings in South Carolina* helped resurrect the focus on Fogle's slaying.

Lieutenant Stivender was quoted in the article, saying, "As the Fogle murder was initially investigated, police investigators identified a person of interest but could never amass enough evidence to seek criminal charges. In the years since, the person of interest moved away and had later died. Investigators hoped that evidence from the initial investigation would be able to link the man to the killing through the use of new DNA technology. It did not."

When the news started circulating, some interesting and curious information was brought to our attention—some that even sounded pretty darn bizarre. A few days after the article appeared in the *Press and Standard*, Corporal Johnson received a call from a lady in Florida who had lived in Walterboro when Elaine was murdered. She had continued receiving the *Press and Standard* and had read the article. She gave him the name of a former police officer who had been engaged to a female police officer. She knew that he also had an interest in Elaine. She remembered him leaving Walterboro shortly after Elaine was murdered.

Around this same time, another tip came in from someone who lived in Walterboro when Elaine was murdered and gave the same name and information of this police officer. She, too, remembered him abruptly leaving after Elaine was killed.

Then a third person called and offered more information on this same person.

We certainly thought this person was worth checking out. We found that he was living in another state. Corporal Johnson contacted the police department in that area. He spoke to an officer who knew this person, and the officer reported that he had some past offenses, mainly code violations and a criminal sexual conduct with a minor charge. His dad had recently passed away, and he was taking care of his mom. His fingerprints were on file, but not his DNA.

The officer he talked to was ready to assist in any way and even offered to rummage through his trash to get his DNA if needed. And he did just that. In a few days, he called, saying he had confiscated some of this person's trash and some of his chewing gum if we needed it for DNA purposes. He would secure it for us if we needed it down the line.

Then we got sidetracked when I got a strange call from Elaine's friend Billy O'Bryant. He had received a letter in the mail that was postmarked in Georgia. The contents were a press release photo of Elaine and a note saying, "You know who this is. Do the right thing!"

Corporal Johnson and I met with Billy at Walterboro Police Department the next day. He brought the letter but said he had no idea who sent it or why. We had him look through some old photo albums that belonged to Elaine to possibly recognize anyone who he remembered while he was at the residence visiting with Nancy and Elaine. He didn't remember them socializing much with anyone at home and didn't recognize anyone, since it had been so long ago. He was asked to give a DNA sample, and he voluntary submitted a buccal swab.

A few days after meeting with Billy, Corporal Johnson received a call from Joseph Flowers Jr., who was the son of Dr. Flowers, the physician Elaine had worked for. He said he got the same letter with the press release photo of Elaine and a note saying, "You know who this is. Do the right thing!"

Corporal Johnson met with Mr. Flowers at his office in Hilton Head, South Carolina. He, too, had no idea who had sent the letter or why. He said that he was only sixteen years old when Elaine died, and he really didn't know much about her. He remembered that she sometimes babysat for his family, and that was the only contact he really had with her. He was asked to give a DNA sample, and he voluntarily submitted a buccal swab.

Corporal Johnson and I agreed on who we thought had sent the letters and handled it promptly and professionally. That ended that little stunt, and we wasted no more time on it.

At this point in the new investigation we had confirmed: 1) An unknown male DNA profile was developed from the panties. 2) These panties were the ones on the couch in the room of the attack and belonged to the victim, Elaine Fogle. 3) Corporal Johnson had collected buccal swabs from some potential male persons of interest that could be compared to the male contributor of the mixed DNA from the panties.

On July 22, 2015, following these findings, some of the evidence returned from SLED to Walterboro in 2014 was submitted to the Beaufort County DNA lab. It would assist with the reevaluation of pertinent evidence in the case, since Beaufort County Lab could possibly have a dramatically shorter turnaround than SLED.

Among the items were the panties from which the mixed DNA had been developed by SLED in 2010 and the recent buccal swabs of potential suspects collected by Corporal Johnson. Even though we had the mixed DNA profile from the panties, we still continued our search for the semen swabs from the autopsy. The semen could perhaps provide a full DNA profile, which could give a better probability of returning a match from the CODIS database.

We contacted SLED DNA lab supervisor lieutenant Robin Taylor and asked if Corporal Johnson and I could meet with her to discuss the details of this case and inform her of where we were in the investigation.

On July 30, 2015, Corporal Johnson and I met with Lieutenant Robin Taylor and DNA Analyst Laura Hash (formerly Laura Mills), who had performed the DNA analysis of the resubmitted evidence from Agent Natalie Crosland in 2010. During the meeting, we learned that there were no records to show that the vaginal, rectal and oral swabs were ever submitted to SLED's chemistry lab.

I informed them of the log-in ledger books that were used in 1978 that documented all evidence signed in for laboratory analysis. Lieutenant Taylor stated that she was not aware of the log-in ledgers, as she was not with SLED in 1978, but she would have additional searching done to try to locate the missing semen swabs.

I checked with several of the former SLED log-in personnel who would remember the ledger books in 1978. They remembered SLED's evidence log-in procedure and how it worked. They assured me that if they had received the semen swabs from the investigator, they would have been entered and documented in the log-in ledger and the card file and then transferred to the appropriate unit for analysis.

I contacted SLED forensic administration Major Todd Hughey and Captain Emily Reinhart and briefed them on details of Elaine's case and that we were examining every avenue to try to locate the semen swabs that should have been submitted to SLED in 1978. I asked if I could meet with them and perform a visual search of the ledger entries on the dates around the incident date of May 27, 1978. It might reveal information of the semen swabs being submitted to SLED around July 5, 1978.

Major Hughey and Captain Reinhart were not at SLED in 1978, so they were not aware of the chemistry log-in procedures or log-in ledgers then. They did advise that over the years some files and records had been microfilmed and digitized and stored in an archive area away from SLED headquarters called Iron Mountain. Captain Reinhart checked with the SLED DNA lab. The old ledgers were not in the lab, so she would initiate a search at Iron Mountain. Captain Reinhart also began reviewing a significant amount of information, files and notes on Elaine's case and carefully tracked the items that remained in question.

Corporal Johnson and I did another thorough search of Walterboro Police Department files for any information that we might have missed that could help in locating the semen swabs. We found nothing new.

It had been several years since I had conferred with Dr. Frank Trefny, the pathologist who was at the crime scene and performed Elaine's autopsy. I reached out to him and informed him of Elaine's case now being actively investigated. I asked for his assistance with any information that might prove helpful.

We were especially interested in the color photos that he had taken at the crime scene and at Elaine's autopsy, as no autopsy photos were located in the files. The only ones in the file were black and white photos of the crime scene. The color photos would show higher quality details of Elaine's injuries. Since it had been so long ago, he wasn't sure if he still had the photos from the scene and autopsy, but he said he would search and get back to me.

Early the next morning, he called and informed me that he had found the crime scene and autopsy photos. He said that his wife overheard our conversation the night before, and when he got off the phone, she told him, "You know, you have a lot of old teaching files on a top shelf in the garage. Maybe Elaine's photos are there."

This took me back to Corporal Johnson's wife giving him the info from my book on Elaine's case. We were indeed very thankful for wives at this time. This was, for sure, another hand to God moment.

Dr. Trefny had photographed the scene and autopsy with 35-millimeter color slide film and graciously offered to meet with us and project the slides to discuss each photo in depth. He even brought his personal slide projector from the '70s, and it still worked like a charm. I guess you could say this was the old-school method of modern-day PowerPoint.

He projected every slide and meticulously explained every image. He allowed us to borrow his slides to have copies made for our files.

We inquired about any knowledge that he might have concerning the missing semen swabs, as we did have his documentation of transferring them to SLED agent Chad Caldwell on July 5, 1978. He said he met with

Agent Caldwell and discussed Elaine's case numerous times in 1978, and he distinctly remembered releasing the semen swabs to him to submit to the SLED chemistry lab.

We periodically checked with the SLED forensic lab about any progress on locating the semen swabs and the log-in ledgers. There was none.

17

A Bombshell

Three Months into the New Investigation, August 2015

For three months, Corporal Johnson and I had been through Elaine's files over and over, communicating every day and sometimes into the night. We cleared every potential suspect, discredited every rumor and cleared every suspect documented in the case file, including Ronald Allen, the suspect from day one.

One statement that Corporal Johnson had always been curious about was the one on file from the employee at the Colleton County Medical Center to Lieutenant Jack Watson in 2005, stating that Ronald Allen's former wife, Fran, had told her that she thought her husband, Ron, might have killed Elaine. Corporal Johnson located Fran in a neighboring town and asked to meet with her.

He told her the statement, and when she heard that the employee referred to Ron as "Bear," she quickly replied, "Ron was called Hammer, not Bear. I do not know this woman, and I never said anything to anyone about Ron being the killer."

She told Corporal Johnson that she did remember a time around 2005 when she got a call from the detective who always accused Ron of being Elaine's killer. He was the detective who she and Ron had talked to on the morning of Elaine's murder. She told Corporal Johnson that she informed this detective of the Black man they had seen washing at the spigot in their yard earlier that morning. She described the investigator as arrogant. He told her emphatically that the case was solved, and Ron was indeed the killer.

She said that Ron finally left Walterboro and went to Tennessee, where his mother lived, because he was constantly being labeled as Elaine's killer. Fran was in nursing school at that time, so she did not go with him.

Fran's interview led Corporal Johnson to an inescapable conclusion: despite all of the hard work the original investigative team had done, it was clear that they suffered from tunnel vision—a single focus on the wrong man. Corporal Johnson told me, "We are not going to let that happen again."

So now we did another total refocus. Was the killer someone the original detectives had never even considered or questioned? At this point, we had eliminated all of the original suspects, and we didn't have a new one. We held on to the belief that the major key to solving the case would come from the mixed DNA from Elaine's panties. We had also been informed by the SLED DNA analyst that mixed DNA profiles generate the lowest percentage of hits in the CODIS national database. This meant that even if Elaine's killer's DNA profile had been entered in CODIS at some point, there was the possibility that it would not return a hit on the mixed DNA profile.

As it turned out, Elaine's case was no exception. CODIS failed to return a match to the mixed DNA.

All of our attempts to locate any records or documentation of the missing semen swabs collected from Elaine during her autopsy were exhausted. These swabs could have provided a complete DNA profile, which would give a stronger probability of generating a hit from CODIS.

Although Elaine's case was further along now than it had been for thirty-seven years, we still had frustrating moments when time just seemed to stop. But the word *stop* was not an option for Corporal Johnson and me. That missing link had to be out there somewhere.

On August 20, 2015, around 9:30 a.m., I was getting into my morning and walking around the house. I asked myself, "Where do we go from here?" Where I went was back to the beginning—to day one in my office at SLED, May 30, 1978, when Elaine's case first came across my desk. I focused on the photographs of the crime scene and latent fingerprints and palm prints that had been lifted from the crime scene and that I had photographed and filed in Elaine's case file.

A light bulb came on in my head.

I threw up my hands thinking, "Oh, my God. We have been so focused on finding the original semen swabs and any DNA that fingerprints and palm prints have never been the concentration."

I immediately called my good buddy SLED latent print examiner Tom Darnell. Tom and I had worked together at SLED since 1990. I briefed him on Elaine's case and told him that Corporal Johnson and I were actively working on it again. He replied, "You know, I remember you talking about this case forever over the years and how it had touched you so deeply. What can I do to help?"

I told him that I had photographed finger and palm prints that were lifted from the crime scene in 1978 and the negative and photos should still be in Elaine's case file folder in the metal file cabinets in the old SLED photography file area. While we were speaking, he was already checking computer records on the case, as most older case information had now been digitized to make it quickly accessible.

Within seconds, he was able to let me know that there was still information on Elaine's case, and yes, the old metal file cabinets with the original photography files were still in the forensic lab area. The negatives and photographs had not been microfilmed or digitized.

He was already ahead of me when I asked if he would check Elaine's files for any finger or palm prints that might still be available for us to enter in AFIS to search for a possible match. Knowing Tom and his passion for his work and getting the bad guy, I could feel the excitement in his voice when he said, "I'm heading that way right now to check the file. Be back to you shortly." I was beyond anxious at this point.

Within the hour, I got a call back from Tom, and he was rushing. "Rita, there was a polaroid negative of a palm print that was lifted from a table from the crime scene in the photography file, and it was still good quality. I had AFIS operator Hayes Baylor enter it into AFIS, and she just got a positive hit back on the palm print. His name is James Willie Butterfield, a fifty-eight-year-old Black male."

This was another hand to God moment. We finally had a name to work with. This was big. I was over the moon. Tom asked if I had ever heard that name or seen it in the case files. I had not, and his description was unexpected to me, as the focus had always been on a White male. Even the profile of a suspect in 1989 noted a White male.

I asked him to call Corporal Johnson right away with the information of the AFIS hit, as he might know the name. In a matter of minutes, Corporal Johnson called me, and no surprise, his first word was, "Wow."

Corporal Johnson knew the name James Willie Butterfield quite well. In 2002, when he worked with the Colleton County Sheriff's Office, he had arrested Willie Butterfield for the attack and assault of a lady. At the

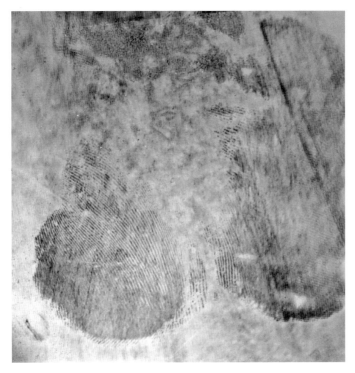

Above: Elaine Fogle photography case file, where palm print and fingerprints from the crime scene were filed for thirty-seven years. *Courtesy of SLED.*

Left: Willie Butterfield's palm print from the end table near the front door. *Elaine Fogle case file.*

time of the attack, Willie Butterfield lived across the street from the victim and knew her. He actually walked by the house when law enforcement was present on the scene. One of the officers informed investigators that they might want to question him. Butterfield was questioned, and investigators observed what appeared to be blood on his jeans and in his mustache.

Corporal Johnson, who was an investigator for the Colleton County Sheriff's office at the time, swabbed the blood in Butterfield's mustache and sent it to SLED for testing. It was a positive match to the victim's blood, which placed Butterfield at the scene and in contact with her blood.

Corporal Johnson recollected that the victim had been beaten in the head with a lamp, which he found interesting. Elaine had been beaten with multiple objects of opportunity, one of which included a lamp, which could show the same MO (modus operandi—particular manner in which a crime is committed) of Elaine's attack.

Johnson also remembered that the lady had reported, "The man that attacked me told me, 'If you don't do what I say I will kill you, 'cause I've already killed one woman.'"

Tom contacted us later in the day with more good news. Two fingerprints that were also a positive match to Willie Butterfield had been returned from AFIS. These were the fingerprints lifted from the broken window at the point of entry.

Tom and I were never at a loss for words. So many times, we talked and shared our successful "war stories." This was definitely another "we got him" moment.

Butterfield's background check revealed that he had an extensive arrest record dating to 1979. His rap sheet showed that he had been in and out of jail through the years since then. Corporal Johnson remembered seeing Willie Butterfield's name one time when he first looked through Elaine's file in an incident report from March 1979. Butterfield had been arrested for the rape of a nineteen-year-old female.

Noted in the incident report, the victim stated that she was walking to her mother's house and a pickup truck passed her several times and then came back and stopped. It was someone she knew, Willie Butterfield. He pulled out a gun and made her get into the truck. He took her to a wooded area, made her take off all her clothes and raped her. Afterward, he tied her feet together and told her, "I just might kill you before this is all over." After that, she said he just got back in his truck and left her there. She later somehow made her way to her mother's house, and she reported her attack to the Colleton County Sheriff's Office.

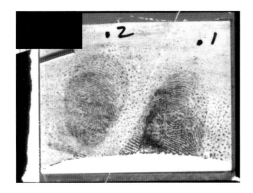

Left: Willie Butterfield's fingerprints on glass from broken window. *Elaine Fogle case file.*

Below: Willie Butterfield mug shot, 1979. *Elaine Fogle case file.*

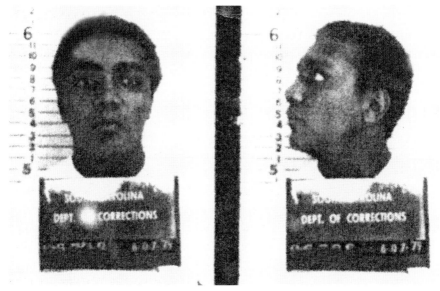

This attack was approximately ten months after Elaine's murder and assault in 1978. Willie Butterfield was twenty years old at the time of this attack. He was five feet, eleven inches tall and weighed 185 pounds.

Corporal Johnson didn't know if Willie Butterfield was still around, but he did know that some of the Butterfield family still lived in Walterboro. He made contact with Butterfield's sister, and she told him that her brother was in a mental facility in Columbia, South Carolina.

Checking further, Corporal Johnson found that Willie Butterfield had been arrested by SLED in Walterboro in April 2010. He was fifty-three years old when he and twenty-eight-year-old Debra Allen were charged with the unauthorized removal of a dead body, desecration of human remains and grand larceny. The report on file revealed that the daughter of eighty-three-year-old Willie Singleton Sr. had previously contacted the Colleton County Sheriff's Office and reported her father was missing.

On March 26, 2010, Colleton County sheriff's deputies and Walterboro police officers discovered Mr. Singleton's vehicle, a Mercury Grand Marquis sedan at the Cambridge Pointe apartments on Nyle Street. While searching the vehicle, they found Mr. Singleton's body in the trunk.

It was not immediately established whether Mr. Singleton was already dead when he was placed in the trunk.

Further investigation revealed that Mr. Singleton had died at a local Colleton County motel on or about March 19, 2010, while in the presence of Butterfield and Allen. They then placed his dead body in the trunk.

Debra Allen was charged with grand larceny and being in possession of Mr. Singleton's vehicle and driving it to the Nyle Street address. In April 2010, Willie Butterfield was charged after he confessed to placing Mr. Singleton, who was already deceased, in the trunk of the car and implicated Ms. Allen in the crime.

In July 2013, Butterfield was in court on these charges and other unrelated charges, which had also happened in 2010.

Prior to the 2013 court hearing, a Blair competency evaluation, which is a mental assessment to determine if a defendant has the mental capacity to understand the charges against him and assist in his own defense (*State of South Carolina vs. Blair*, 1981), was conducted on Butterfield. The results of the evaluation determined that Butterfield was not mentally competent to stand trial in his part of assisting Ms. Allen in Mr. Singleton's murder and putting his body in the trunk of the car. This court ruling resulted in Willie Butterfield being committed to the Crafts-Farrow State Mental facility in Columbia, South Carolina, following the hearing.

Wille Butterfield, 2012. *Elaine Fogle case file.*

A bizarre note in this case was that Ms. Allen was never able to be tried in a court of law either. While awaiting trial, she was hit by a car crossing a road and was killed.

Although we now had palm prints and fingerprints found at the crime scene positively identified to Willie Butterfield, there were still some concerns. The prints did place Willie Butterfield in Elaine's house at some point but did not prove that he sexually assaulted and killed Elaine.

We did have the partial male DNA profile from the panties from the crime scene, but at this point, we did not know who it belonged to. A DNA sample from Willie Butterfield would be needed to determine if the male DNA found on the panties from the crime scene matched Butterfield's DNA. The SLED DNA lab would perform the DNA analysis once it got a standard DNA from Willie Butterfield. The lab would also need the panties back from Walterboro for a reanalysis, but that presented a slight problem. The panties were still in evidence at Beaufort County's DNA lab after being submitted by Walterboro Police Department in July 2015.

SLED chief Mark Keel was briefed on the progress of the case, and he contacted Walterboro chief Wade Marvin to get the evidence back from Beaufort for the SLED DNA lab to perform the analysis. On August 27, 2015, SLED flew Analyst Laura Hash by helicopter to Beaufort County Sheriff's Office to pick up all evidence that would be needed for the additional analysis of the DNA profile.

On September 3, 2015, Corporal Johnson and Lieutenant Stivender interviewed Willie Butterfield at the mental facility in Columbia and collected a buccal swab that would provide his DNA standard for testing. That same day, Corporal Johnson submitted Butterfield's buccal swab to the SLED DNA lab for comparison analysis with the DNA from the panties.

It had taken thirty-seven years to get to this point, and we felt certain that we had what we needed but waiting for the DNA results seemed to last forever.

And then it happened. The thirty-seven years of waiting was over. On September 18, 2015, at 10:36 a.m., I received a text from Corporal Johnson: "We gotta match on Butterfield. Call you later."

I threw my hands up, "Yes, yes, we got him!" I was on pins and needles waiting to hear the details.

About five minutes later, I got the call from Corporal Johnson saying, "Wow, Willie Butterfield is our guy. Just got a call from Analyst Hash at SLED informing me that Butterfield's DNA was a match to the male contributor of the mixed DNA on the panties."

I came out with a "wow" this time and got a big chuckle from Corporal Johnson on that comeback. He told me that he still had to meet with Deputy Solicitor Sean Thornton with the results and have him instruct on how to move forward with charging Willie Butterfield for Elaine's murder and assault.

The news from Solicitor Thornton was not what we wanted to hear at first. He said that even though we had the palm print, fingerprints and a DNA match to Butterfield, which was probable cause for his arrest, he needed to go one step further to make sure everything was covered because Butterfield submitted the buccal swab while he was deemed incompetent.

Solicitor Thornton said that if Willie Butterfield's DNA was available from any arrests prior to him being declared incompetent in 2013, that DNA could be used for the comparison of DNA from the panties.

Records showed that when Willie Butterfield was arrested in 2010 for the unauthorized removal of a dead body and desecration of human remains, his DNA was collected, and his profile was entered in the CODIS DNA database. So, this assured that Butterfield had not yet been deemed incompetent when his DNA was originally collected. This 2010 arrest was also when his palm prints and fingerprints were entered in the AFIS fingerprint database.

With Willie Butterfield's DNA profile from 2010 now on file at SLED, Solicitor Thornton contacted SLED DNA analyst Laura Hash and gave her instructions to proceed with the testing of Willie Butterfield's DNA from 2010 to the DNA on the panties.

Corporal Johnson and I remained positive that the reanalysis would also be a match to Butterfield, but we didn't stop working. We knew that the more evidence there is to work with on a case the better. The missing semen swabs could certainly help now by providing additional DNA from the scene since we finally had a suspect to compare it to. We thought it might be worth another try to check on any progress the SLED chemistry lab might have made on locating the evidence log-in ledgers.

Examiner Tom Darnell had already informed me that the crime scene, latent print, firearms and photography lab log-in ledgers were in the latent print lab area at SLED. They were never sent out to the archive area, Iron Mountain.

I contacted SLED captain Rinehart to check if any progress had been made in locating the ledgers, and she had good news. They had located the box number where the ledgers were at Iron Mountain, and they were having them sent back to SLED for future reference and safekeeping. I again inquired if it might be possible for Corporal Johnson and me to go to SLED headquarters and view the ledgers when they had them in the lab to check for any entries of the semen swabs. She said it might be a possibility and would get back to me.

We were aware that it would take a while to get the final DNA results that were needed to positively confirm if Willie Butterfield was our man from Analyst Hash, but we certainly didn't plan on a storm of the century hitting South Carolina and devastating the entire state for weeks.

Beginning on October 1, 2015, continuous rain, flooding and devastation hit the entire state of South Carolina, hour after hour and day after day. It devastated the state with twenty-four-plus inches of rain before it finally stopped. Many highways, streets and homes were underwater. Dams broke and sent more water to already-suffering areas. By the time the last raindrop was counted, the October 2015 storm went down in history as one of the most prolific rainfall events in the modern history of the United States.

SLED was shut down for more than a week, so the final analysis of Butterfield's DNA and the panties was on hold until SLED was able to resume normal work schedules after the storm.

In the interim, while waiting on the final results from Analyst Hash, Corporal Johnson and I proceeded with our progress notes and documentation of our findings from May 2015 to the present. On October 22, 2015, Corporal Johnson informed me that he had received the final DNA results from Analyst Hash per her instructions from Solicitor Thornton, and Willie Butterfield was a positive match. Her final report read:

> The DNA profile developed from item 26.1(cuttings from panties) is a mixture of at least two individuals. Elaine Fogle and James Willie Butterfield cannot be excluded as possible contributors to this mixture.
> The Y-STR (male contributor) profile developed from item 26.1.1 (cuttings from panties) matches the Y-STR DNA profile developed from James Willie Butterfield. The probability of randomly selecting an unrelated male individual having a Y-STR profile matching this item is approximately 1 in 8,600.

This was another wow moment for both of us, but excited as we were and as much as we wanted to tell the world, Solicitor Thornton imposed a gag order until he gave Corporal Johnson the go-ahead to make official charges against Butterfield after all the legal issues were finalized. The gag order prevented us from informing Elaine's family. We were sad about that because we were so ready to let them know the news. They had been waiting for so long.

Corporal Johnson and I were double sad, as October 25 was Elaine's sister's birthday. We were hoping we could give Eolean the happiest birthday present she could ask for since Elaine's death. We weren't able to do that.

After the completion of all of the legal procedures, James Willie Butterfield was charged with murder, criminal sexual conduct first degree and burglary first degree. Now, after thirty-seven years, Elaine's family would finally get the answers and news that they had longed to hear and, most of all, the peace that they have always wanted.

Corporal Johnson contacted Eolean, Melissa and Elaine's cousin James to let them know that we had an important update on Elaine's case and asked them to meet with us at the Walterboro Police Department. They had been disappointed so many times over the years, and they were anxious to hear any news.

December 1, 2015, was a beautiful sunny morning in South Carolina's Lowcountry. I was so excited that we could finally inform Elaine's family of the news of an arrest for Elaine's murder. My ride to Walterboro was peaceful and calming. On the way, I stopped and picked up two red roses.

When everyone was present in the room, we all gave hugs to the family, and for a brief moment, the room went totally silent. The family had no idea what was coming next. Chief Marvin and Corporal Johnson humbly addressed the family and delivered the news that they had arrested the man who murdered Elaine. We all had an emotional overflow, and everybody teared up, including Chief Marvin and Corporal Johnson.

I took Eolean's hand, hugged her and handed her one of the roses saying, "This one is for you. You now finally have the peace that you have always wanted. We got him!" Then I handed her the other rose and said, "And this one is for Elaine. You can rest now sweet girl. We got him!" Tears turned into smiles and pleasant conversation.

As we departed, Corporal Johnson turned to me and said, "This is a very good day for me."

And to him I said, "My personal quest for thirty-seven years to see Elaine's murder solved has finally ended. Thank you, my friend." This wonderful, dedicated and compassionate man did something that no one had done. He didn't stop. He didn't put the case back on the shelf.

I spent the rest of the day with Elaine's family. There was no doubt that Elaine us was right there with us. She and her mom and dad were smiling down on us. We enjoyed a tasty Lowcounty lunch, which, of course, included sweet tea, collards, corn bread and fried chicken. We chatted about a lot of what we had shared and gone through to get to this day. Good, bad and ugly, no matter what, we had stuck together, and here we were, still together. That would never change.

In the peacefulness at my home that evening, I opened Elaine's files once again. I stared at the photo of the panties on the couch and the photos of the palm print and fingerprints. These were the final pieces of the puzzle. Goose bumps crawled all over me as I thought that I walked around that palm print and the fingerprints in the photography lab every day for twenty-four and a half years during my tenure at SLED. They were within arm's length all the time. They were sleeping through the last thirty-seven years. They just had to be woken up, and we did it.

The following day, December 2, 2015, Walterboro chief Wade Marvin issued a press release charging James Willie Butterfield with murder, criminal sexual conduct first degree and burglary first degree. He reported that information leading to identifying Butterfield had been double and triple checked, so he assured the public that the police was 100 percent sure of the evidence match to James Willie Butterfield. He also said that although James Willie Butterfield was in custody awaiting a bond hearing, he was innocent until proven guilty by a court of law.

It was an especially good day for the residents of Walterboro and all who knew Elaine. They could now be at peace that Elaine's murderer was arrested and incarcerated, though it was upsetting that he was in a mental facility rather than a regular jail cell. The one positive of this was that he was not out in the general population and could not hurt anyone ever again.

Social, local and state media were abuzz covering the news of Elaine's cold case. It brought back to me the comment Eolean told me that Elaine would say: "When I die, I'm gonna make history."

The next day, December 3, 2015, front-page headlines in the *Press and Standard* read, "Charges Filed in 37-Year Old Murder." It was followed the next day with an editorial headlined "Closing a Cold Case." Reporter George Salsberry's editorials gave the citizens of Walterboro an understanding of how Elaine Fogle's case had unfolded in the last several months and was finally solved:

> Corporal Gean Johnson was assigned to review the massive case file in May of this year, near the anniversary date of the murder 37 years ago. Johnson began making headway with new leads.
>
> Over the course of the investigation, James Willie Butterfield became the primary suspect through evidence collected from the original crime scene.
>
> The closure of this case would not be possible without the hard work and investigative skills of the original case officers and SLED agents who assisted, and preserved evidence over time.
>
> Retired SLED Agent Rita Shuler never gave up on the Fogle case. She was there in the beginning and she was there when it ended.
>
> Shuler said shortly after Corporal Johnson was assigned the case, he called her and asked if she would consider assisting him, telling her

that Police Chief Wade Marvin had given his authorization to have her involved, even though she was no longer an active law enforcement officer.

Shuler quickly found that she had met a kindred spirit in the quest. "Corporal Johnson said he would stick with it. That man did some work. He didn't stop. It just needed somebody to stay on it, not just blink and put it back on the shelf. We had to go back to old-school techniques, so it was a mixture of old and new. We had to wake up the old files and bring them up to date with the new technology. There we found the main threads that we needed in the mountain of evidence and started pulling on them."

After that Johnson and Shuler pulled others into the case to finalize the results. Former and current SLED agents and forensic analysts assisted to finalize the results of the evidence.

The December 3, 2015 edition of the Charleston *Post and Courier* headline read, "Preserving Evidence Key to Arrest in 1978 Case." Reporter Dave Munday wrote:

The family of Gwendolyn Elaine Fogle never gave up hope that her killer would one day be found. They broke down in tears Tuesday when police announced they had made an arrest, and that James Willie Butterfield was charged with murder, first-degree criminal sexual conduct and first-degree burglary.

The keys to the arrest were preserving evidence collected at the crime scene until technology caught up with it, and assigning a dogged investigator and retired SLED agent to sift through it until they could nail a suspect.

Family members were called to the Walterboro Police Department Tuesday to be told about the arrest.

James Fogle, Elaine's cousin said, "We just sat there in silence for a few minutes. We've been waiting on this for thirty-seven years. The reaction was just tearful. It's not about us, it's about Elaine. Elaine was a good person. She didn't have any enemies. It's just a shame that happened to her. I know it's not over 'til he's in the slammer, but we can have some peace of mind now."

After years of dead ends, Chief Wade Marvin assigned the case to investigator, Corporal Gean Johnson in May.

Corporal Johnson said, "This is the first time I have ever taken home work. I lost track of the hours spent at night going through the case files, but I felt like I owned it to the family. The case needed a new set of eyes and someone to stay on it!"

Johnson worked closely with Rita Shuler, a retired forensic photographer with SLED. She had helped keep the case alive. She included Elaine's unsolved case in one of her books she had written on crimes in South Carolina, "Small-Town Slayings in South Carolina."

Shuler says, "Thank God, for the evidence that was preserved. That was the key to solving this case."

The December 3, 2015 edition of Elaine's hometown Orangeburg, South Caroline newspaper, the *Times and Democrat*, headlines read, "Man Charged in 1978 Murder of Orangeburg Native." Reporter Martha Rose Brown wrote:

Persistence and DNA evidence have led investigators to a suspect believed to be responsible for the 1978 slaying of Orangeburg native Gwendolyn Elaine Fogle.

James Willie Butterfield, 59 years old of Walterboro has been charged with murder, first-degree criminal sexual conduct and first-degree burglary in connection with Fogle's murder.

James Fogle said the case of his first cousin's slaying took on new momentum this past May when Walterboro Police Investigator Gean Johnson "took the case by the horns."

Fogle said in 1999, he started gathering his own file of reports and information on the case and contacted Walterboro Police Department and SLED to try and keep the case moving.

He was with Elaine's sister, Eolean, which is the only living immediate family member when investigators met with them to announce Butterfield's arrest.

Retired SLED Agent/Forensic photographer, Rita Shuler, formerly of the Providence Community of Orangeburg County, worked on the case when it happened in 1978. Shuler was consulted to assist the Walterboro Police Department with the new investigation.

She had maintained contact with members of Elaine's family through the years, and featured the case in one of her books she has authored on South Carolina cases.

Included in the article were memories of several of Elaine's cousins who still lived in the Orangeburg area. What they remembered most about Elaine was her kindness, that she was such a beautiful person who would do anything in the world for anyone.

During all of this media frenzy, Corporal Johnson called me to tell me of an interesting happening. He said, "I was buzzed from the front entrance office of the police department, and was informed that there were some ladies that wanted to speak to me. I figured it was someone else that might need assistance with a situation. Well, I soon found out, it wasn't that. When I opened the door, they started blasting me about arresting their brother, Willie Butterfield."

It was Willie Butterfield's sisters, saying, "No way my brother did this, and why didn't you let us know before I had to see it in the newspaper and on television?"

I chuckled because I knew he handled it, but I had to ask, "What did you say?"

His reply, "Wow! Ms. Rita, I just told them that I understand your concern for your brother, but we have the evidence, fingerprints and DNA from the scene that confirms that your brother, Willie, did this. Any more questions?" At that point, after they said a few more verbal remarks that weren't very nice, Corporal Johnson said they turned away and left.

18.

BOND HEARING

December 2015

On December 14, 2015, a bond hearing for Willie Butterfield was held during the Colleton County General Sessions Court. He was transported to the Colleton County Courthouse from Crafts-Farrow, the state mental health facility in Columbia, South Carolina, where he was housed.

Butterfield, in handcuffs and shackles, nonchalantly walked into the courtroom with a South Carolina Department of Mental Health public safety officer. The look on his face was like he didn't have a care in the world. With his guard sitting next to him, he took a seat on the top row of the jury box, joining other inmates who would also go before the judge that day for bond hearing, possible guilty pleas and motions for bail reduction. The other inmates, dressed in their orange jumpsuits, stood out from Butterfield, as he was dressed in his normal, everyday casual attire.

Elaine's sister and Melissa had traveled 150 miles, two and a half hours, from their home in Clinton, South Carolina, to attend the bond hearing. Mr. Butterfield had gotten a free ride with meals included.

I was sitting with Eolean and Melissa, and this was the first time we had seen Willie Butterfield in person. He seemed very disinterested in what was going on in the courtroom proceedings and just kept looking around and out at the courtroom crowd with his deep hollow eyes. It sickened me to think that he was the last thing Elaine had seen in the final minutes of her life.

I took a deep breath and focused on his hands. Even though he was in handcuffs, he held on to his hands, slowly rolling them around and around.

Willie Butterfield in court, 2015.
Courtesy of the Press and Standard.

Chills and disgust went through me. These were the hands that so brutally attacked and bludgeoned Elaine Fogle to death, and to make sure his job was done, he took those hands and wrapped that fire poker around her neck.

He ended the life of an innocent sweet girl who never did anything to him, yet he got to live the years that followed and continue to do bad acts all along the way.

So many times during the investigation, the word *strong* came up, alluding that the person who did this had to be very strong to bend the iron fire poker around Elaine's neck. He was physically strong, perhaps, back then, but today, seeing Butterfield for the first time, I thought this evil person was the epitome of weakness.

Silent thoughts filled my head: Oh, you must have felt so big back then, wiping your hands as you left Elaine's house that night when you threw her jeans up on the porch roof. I bet you were thinking, "Well, I'm done with that!" Mr. Butterfield, these are the same hands that left your palm print and fingerprints in Elaine's home when you murdered and raped her. Those hands that caused an unspeakable horror to Elaine were the same hands that left a silent witness at her murder scene. You had no idea that you left your signature for us that night. Those prints were yours and gave us your name. You had no knowledge or thoughts that no two people have the same fingerprints, palm prints or footprints. They are only unique to one person, and in this case, Mr. Butterfield, that person is you. You signed your name to one of the most brutal and horrific crimes in the state of South Carolina's history—one that this charming Lowcountry town of Walterboro and the state of South Carolina would rather not claim. Residents in Walterboro never forgot that night, and they never will. Many still say as they speak of it, "We never thought something like this would happen in a small town like ours." You got away with so much evil for decades in your life, and now you're old and evaluations show that you are not mentally competent to stand trial for your crimes. Somehow, the scales of justice just don't seem to balance with that.

Melissa leaned over and whispered to me, "He gives me the creeps."

It was almost two hours before Willie Butterfield's name was called to go before Judge R. Lawton McIntosh for his bond hearing on the charges of murder, first-degree burglary and first-degree criminal sexual conduct. He was surrounded by the Department of Mental Health Public Safety officer and Colleton County sheriff deputies as he stood in front of Judge R. Lawton McIntosh.

Fourteenth Circuit Court solicitor Duffie Stone addressed Judge McIntosh and told him that Willie Butterfield had been incarcerated in the Crafts-Farrow mental health facility in Columbia, South Carolina, since 2012, because at that time, he was deemed incompetent to stand trial on numerous criminal charges in Colleton County. He stated that Willie Butterfield was appearing in court without legal counsel and that the Colleton County public defender's office was asked to represent Butterfield at least through the bond hearing.

Solicitor Stone stated that Willie Butterfield was arrested and charged earlier in the month for the May 28, 1978 rape and murder of Gwendolyn Elaine Fogle in her Walterboro home. The reexamination of evidence in the case revealed that Butterfield's palm and fingerprints and his DNA were found in Elaine Fogle's home at the crime scene. This pointed to Willie Butterfield as the only suspect. Stone gave some history of Butterfield's criminal record through the years. He had served ten years in prison after being found guilty of charges of grand larceny, assault and battery of a high and aggravated nature in 1979; a forgery charge in 1989; and charges of assault and battery of a high and aggravated nature and criminal domestic violence in 1999. Stone stated that Butterfield was ruled competent to stand trial in those cases.

Judge McIntosh then asked if anyone from the families would like to speak. Melissa Hughes, daughter of Elaine's sister, pleaded, "Please don't let him out. Keep him behind bars and away from anybody else that he could hurt. My mother has been afraid for thirty-seven years and that has been long enough. Every time that she would see a stranger or, for that matter, even someone she knew, she would wonder if that was the person that killed her sister."

After hearing the history of Willie Butterfield's criminal history and the plea from Fogle's family, Judge McIntosh ruled that Butterfield be held without bond on the murder charge. In a stark statement, the judge said, "During my time on the bench, I have only allowed one murder suspect bond, and in that case, a man had killed his brother in a fight." The bond hearing was a legal formality, and Butterfield would remain under lock and key at the mental health facility.

It was reported that the last time Willie Butterfield was in Colleton County court was July 16, 2013, when the Blair hearing determined that he was not mentally competent to stand trial, so Solicitor Stone asked the judge to order Butterfield to undergo another mental evaluation before conducting another Blair hearing.

Butterfield's public defender agreed to Stone's motion. After the Blair ruling deeming Butterfield incompetent, the Fourteenth Circuit Court Solicitor's Office moved to dismiss all pending criminal charges against Willie Butterfield that were filed in 2010. These were: April 2010, desecration of human remains and unauthorized removal of a dead body; May 2010, unlawful taking of a firearm and weapon from a law enforcement officer and assault on an employee of a correctional facility; August 2010, first-degree burglary, assault and battery of a high and aggravated nature and kidnapping; and September 2010, two counts of first-degree burglary and single counts of first-degree criminal sexual conduct and kidnapping.

It was also documented that all of these criminal charges could be filed again if new competency examinations determined that Butterfield's mental state had improved to the point that he was competent to stand trial.

An interesting point here is that Butterfield's charges in May, August and September 2010 happened after his arrest in April 2010, which was during the time he was awaiting his court hearing in 2013.

After the hearing, Deputy Solicitor Thornton met with me, Eolean, Melissa and the member of the victim's advocate for the Fourteenth Circuit Solicitor's Office who was assigned to work with the Fogle family at every step of the judicial process and keep them informed of their rights. He discussed the Blair ruling in depth and advised that he would proceed in getting a new mental evaluation scheduled for Butterfield as soon as possible.

Another point of interest that he discussed was looking into a M'Naghten ruling that could possibly apply in this case. The M'Naghten rule focuses on whether a criminal defendant accused of a crime knew the nature of the crime or understood right from wrong at the time it was committed. It was adopted in the U.S. court system in the early 1900s, so it would be a long shot but worth pursuing. As reported in the bond hearing, Butterfield's past criminal records dating to 1979 showed that he was competent to stand trial for a number of those crimes and served time in jail and prison. That documented that when he murdered Elaine in 1978, he was mentally competent. This gave the family some hope that he could possibly stand trial in the future for the charges in Elaine's case even though he was deemed mentally incompetent at the present time.

It was now a waiting period for the legal process to continue.

We were later informed that the M'Naghten rule did not apply in Elaine's case and competency evaluations of Butterfield would continue.

Christmas was only days away. It would be another Christmas that the Fogle family would not have Elaine there to celebrate with them.

In the January 13, 2016 edition of Elaine's sister's hometown newspaper, the *Clinton Chronicle*, headlines read, "Arrest in 37-Year-Old Case May Provide Closure for Clinton Woman." Reporter Vic McDonald wrote:

A 37-year-old weight has been lifted from the shoulders of a family with connections to Clinton and the South Carolina Lowcountry town of Walterboro.

An arrest has been made in connection with the beating and strangulation death of Eolean Hughes', sister Gwendolyn Elaine Fogle who was twenty-six years old when she was murdered.

In December 2015, the Hughes family learned that 59-year-old James Willie Butterfield had been arrested and charged with Elaine's death in 1978.

Mrs. Hughes daughter Melissa says her mother has lived in fear, looking over her shoulder at every person whose eyes might have lingered on her just a moment too long. She would say, "What if that's him, and now he's coming after me!"

Melissa says, "For years I have not seen my mother smile. She has never wanted to put up a Christmas tree. It's always been a small ceramic tree sitting on a table. This year we put up a Christmas tree."

The case was solved by Corporal Gean Johnson and retired SLED Agent and true crime author Rita Shuler.

Mrs. Hughes also credits her cousin James Fogle for his determination on working with the family and contacting Law Enforcement Agencies through the years.

Mrs. Hughes said, "I never really paid attention to true crime shows, but working with her cousin James on gathering information on Elaine's case, I began watching and hoping to pick up tips on how murders are investigated and solved.

It took thirty-seven years to get Elaine's murderer. It was a long time coming, but with it has brought some long-awaited peace for our family."

19

PRELIMINARY HEARING

March 2016

On March 10, 2016, a preliminary hearing for James Willie Butterfield was held at the Colleton County Courthouse. The hearing would determine whether there was enough evidence in the case to require a trial in a Common Pleas Court, which is a higher court for the prosecutor to present the case to a grand jury to seek an indictment.

Eolean, Melissa and I were in the courtroom for the hearing. Members of Willie Butterfield's family were also present. It was an open court proceeding, and some Walterboro residents were there in support of Elaine and her family.

Morrison Payne was the presiding judge. The defendant, Willie Butterfield, was not present at the hearing. Public defender Matthew Walker was there to represent Butterfield. Career criminal solicitor Tameaka Leggett, with the Fourteenth Circuit Solicitor's Office, presented the case.

Solicitor Leggett called Corporal Johnson to the stand and had him take the court through the details of what happened the night in May 27. He went through the timeline of events.

Solicitor Leggett then inquired on the extent of the injuries to Ms. Fogle and the manner of death. Johnson added that after the investigation was reopened in 2015, we met with pathologist Dr. Frank Trefny, who performed Elaine's autopsy in 1978. He said, "Dr. Trefny found the cause of death was strangulation by a fire poker wrapped around Miss Fogle's neck. The manner of death was homicide."

Leggett asked if Dr. Trefny determined whether Miss Fogle was sexually assaulted. "Yes," Johnson said, "Dr. Trefny's results showed that there was extensive vaginal and anal bruising, so she was raped and also sodomized."

Leggett stated that records show that the case had been looked at again and again over a period of thirty-seven years and asked how the accused, Willie Butterfield, became the main suspect in Elaine's assault, rape and murder after Johnson was assigned the case in May 2015.

Johnson replied, "In August 2015, SLED latent print examiner Tom Darnell was contacted and asked to check the original 1978 SLED photography case file for any prints that could be entered into the AFIS database. He located photos of palm prints and fingerprints in the file and entered them into the AFIS fingerprint database. A positive match from AFIS was returned on a palm print and two fingerprints that belonged to James Willie Butterfield."

Leggett then asked about the DNA that was also matched to Butterfield. Corporal Johnson detailed that in 2010 the original evidence from the crime scene was once again resubmitted to SLED to be rechecked using newly advanced technology for DNA. DNA was found on panties belonging to Ms. Fogle that were found on the couch in the living room where the attack occurred. The profile contained Fogle's DNA and an unknown male's DNA. Because Willie Butterfield was now a strong suspect, we learned that his DNA was in CODIS from a previous arrest in 2010. His DNA was compared to the unknown male DNA on the panties on the couch by SLED DNA analyst Laura Hash. The DNA was a positive match to Willie Butterfield's DNA.

At this point, Solicitor Leggett asked Corporal Johnson if he had any knowledge that Fogle and Butterfield knew each other or were acquainted with each other at any time. Johnson said that on September 3, 2015, he and Lieutenant Stivender interviewed Willie Butterfield at the Crafts-Farrow Hospital in Columbia, South Carolina. "We asked him if he knew Elaine Fogle. In the beginning he denied knowing Elaine. We showed him a photo of Elaine and Elaine's house. We asked if he had ever been in Elaine's house, and he said he was never in that house or on that property. We informed him that his palm print and fingerprints were found in that house. After some hesitation, Butterfield came back with, 'Well, yes, I did know her.' When I asked why he did this to Elaine, he said, 'I don't know.' He then abruptly stopped and said he wanted his lawyer. Of course, there is no way of knowing if he was telling the truth about any of this, of actually knowing Ms. Fogle."

Solicitor Leggett had no further questions.

Judge Payne announced that public defendant Matthew Walker would be representing Willie Butterfield. After reflecting on Corporal Johnson's details of the case, Walker asked if Willie Butterfield was a suspect early in the investigation, in 1978.

Johnson replied that after viewing the files and speaking to some of the original investigators, they informed him that Butterfield's prints were on file back then from prior unrelated arrests in Walterboro. They also said that Butterfield's name was on a list of persons of interest in the early stages of the investigation, along with numerous other offenders in the area. This list was sent to SLED, along with their fingerprint cards to be compared to the prints from the crime scene on file in Elaine's case.

Walker asked why there was not a match back then or even through the years when the case was examined again and again if Butterfield's prints were on file and the unknown latent prints inside the house from the scene were also on file.

Corporal Johnson replied, "I can't answer as to why a match wasn't reported to Willie Butterfield back then, as there were no official reports of fingerprint comparisons from SLED in the file from back then."

Proceedings were abruptly halted in the courtroom when Judge Payne called down Butterfield's family for making gestures. She firmly stated, "Ma'am! No more! You can be in the courtroom, but you cannot make faces." The courtroom went totally silent.

Judge Payne addressed Walker to continue. He asked Corporal Johnson, "So, in 2015, the palm print and fingerprints found in the house were a match to Willie Butterfield?"

Johnson replied, "Yes, because of the AFIS fingerprint database now, the negatives and photos of the prints lifted from the scene in 1978 that were on file in the SLED photography case file all through the years were entered into the AFIS database by SLED examiner Tom Darnell. A palm print and two fingerprint matches were returned from AFIS that belonged to Willie Butterfield."

Johnson explained that Willie Butterfield's fingerprints and palm prints had been entered in the AFIS database in 2010 from prior arrests unrelated to Elaine's case. That resulted in the positive hit when the prints from the 1978 crime scene were entered by Darnell in 2015.

Mr. Walker then inquired about the DNA that was matched to Willie Butterfield. Corporal Johnson replied as he had previously to Solicitor Leggett, "In 2010, the evidence from the crime scene was resubmitted to

SLED to be rechecked using the advanced DNA technology. DNA was found on panties belonging to Ms. Fogle, which were found on the couch in the living room where the attack occurred. The profile contained Ms. Fogle's DNA and an unknown male's DNA. Because Willie Butterfield was now a strong suspect, we learned that his DNA was in CODIS from a previous arrest in 2010. His DNA was compared to the unknown male DNA on the panties on the couch, and it was a match to Willie Butterfield."

Mr. Walker asked, "In reference to the autopsy, did it reveal anything about semen being removed from Ms. Fogle's body?"

"Yes," Johnson said, "there were several vials of semen collected. Written documentation was located in the case file showing that Dr. Trefny who performed the autopsy had transferred the vials to SLED agent Chad Caldwell in July 1978, to be submitted to the SLED Forensics Chemistry Lab for testing. From some case file notes, it appeared attempts had been made through the years when the case was looked at again to locate these semen swabs to be retested, but the swabs could not be accounted for. We also attempted on several occasions after reopening the case in 2015 to locate the swabs, and there were no records at SLED that they were ever submitted."

Walker asked if Agent Caldwell was still around to possibly give his memories of this. "Yes, sir," Johnson said. "He is now chief of police of Moncks Corner, South Carolina. I did talk to him, and he said he submitted the vials to SLED."

Walker let out a sigh, "Alright."

When asked whether Butterfield's doctor or caretaker was present in the interview at Crafts-Farrow, Corporal Johnson answered, "No, but we had permission from the facility staff to speak to him. At first, we asked him a few questions not related to the case just to verify he could comprehend what was going on. He seemed to understand, and I told him I wanted to ask him about an old case from Walterboro. I then explained to him that we needed to inform him of his Miranda rights first. We asked if he understood, and if he did to sign his name to the Miranda form. He said he could not read or write. I then read him his rights and showed him the form, but in fact, he did initial on the appropriate lines and signed his name on the appropriate line at the bottom of the Miranda rights form."

At this point, public defender Walker said he had no more questions.

After hearing testimony and the evidence presented in court, Judge Payne ruled that there was enough probable cause for this case to be bound over for common pleas court. Even though that was good news, we knew that Willie Butterfield was still deemed incompetent to stand trial but would continue to undergo periodic competency evaluations.

20.

COMPETENCY HEARING

May 2017

On May 22, 2017, a competency hearing was conducted at the Colleton County Courthouse by Judge Paul Buckner to present the results of Butterfield's competency evaluations over the past months and rule if Butterfield might now be competent to stand trial for his charges in Elaine's case.

Forensic psychiatrist Dr. Matthew Gaskins had been assigned to perform the first competency evaluation on Butterfield following the bond hearing in December 2015. His results of the evaluation showed that he was unable to form a professional opinion on Butterfield's competency because Butterfield was uncooperative and refused to answer questions. He was also not cooperating with the mental facility's staff in his treatment. Some health professionals did have concerns that during the interview he was faking and embellishing on his mental capabilities.

Because Dr. Gaskins was unable to form his opinion on whether Butterfield was mentally capable of assisting in his defense in the trial, Solicitor Sean Thornton requested Judge Buckner to order another evaluation on Butterfield by another forensic psychiatrist.

Butterfield's public defender, Matthew Walker, disagreed with doing another evaluation and stated that the earlier determination that Butterfield was not mentally competent to stand trial was still valid. Solicitor Thornton refuted that, stating that a defendant's mental competency could change over time. Judge Buckner agreed and ordered another evaluation to be done by forensic psychiatrist Dr. Donna Mattox.

In February 2017, Dr. Mattox conducted her mental evaluation with Butterfield. Her results concluded that Willie Butterfield was not mentally competent to stand trial and, in her professional opinion, would likely not be competent in the foreseeable future. She also stated that he would be a danger to the general public.

Based on the findings of both reports, Judge Buckner filed an order for Willie Butterfield to wear an electronic monitor at all times while housed in Crafts-Farrow and confirmed that Butterfield could not be released from the mental facility without an order from the court.

Judge Buckner's final order was that Butterfield's indictments in Elaine Fogle's case—murder, criminal sexual conduct first degree and burglary first degree—would be *nolle prossed* (dismissal of charges by the prosecution). Judge Buckner concluded, "If James Willie Butterfield is ever deemed competent, charges will be filed again, and he could stand trial in the future for the charges."

This person who had been charged with Elaine Fogle's brutal murder and rape, as well as all of his other charges of violence and crime, had now been dismissed of all charges. All through the years, he kept going to jail and kept getting back out. He was free to abuse women and continue on his crime journey throughout his life.

Today, Willie Butterfield has no worries. He will continue to be housed in the state facility and will be taken care of. He might never be punished for all the evil he has done. Once again, the scales of justice just don't seem to balance with that.

ENDING NOTE

Even though Elaine's case is now ruled closed, her family still lives every day with the loss of Elaine. She was taken from them by the evil acts of James Willie Butterfield, but they never forgot her, and they never will. The city and residents of Walterboro, as well, have never healed from the heartbreak of losing one of the town's most loved people, but Elaine will never be forgotten.

Corporal Johnson shared with me, "I wanted to close my law enforcement career as a sheriff or police chief of a smaller agency, but once the Fogle case was solved, I feel that recognition outweighed all and has become the highlight of my career."

For myself, my thirty-seven-year quest of seeing Elaine's case solved finally concluded. Cherished words from her family will always remain with me, "Thank you for giving us hope."

Corporal Johnson and I remain in touch, and we hold on to the hope that one day Willie Butterfield will be deemed competent and his charges for Elaine's murder and sexual assault will be filed again. When that happens, it can be assured that Corporal Gean Johnson will be standing right there to place handcuffs on James Willie Butterfield as soon as he is let out of the facility, and God willing, I will be right there next to him.

Corporal Gean Johnson was awarded 2015 Officer of the Year by Walterboro Police Department for his work with Elaine's case. *Courtesy of Corporal Gean Johnson.*

SLED fingerprint examiner Tom Darnell continues to go the extra mile to get the bad guys of the street. *Courtesy of Tom Darnell.*

One constant in life is change. Over the years, highly advanced forensic technology has brought many changes to law enforcement and, above all, the way forensic evidence is examined. However, let's never forget, it still takes a human to make it work.

BIBLIOGRAPHY

Avant, Travis, in conversation with author.

Caldwell, Chad, in conversation with author.

Caldwell, David, in conversation with author.

Crosland, Natalie, in conversation with author.

Darnell, Tom (SLED fingerprint examiner), in conversation with author.

Gwendolyn Elaine Fogle case files. South Carolina Law Enforcement Division.

Gwendolyn Elaine Fogle case files. Walterboro Police Department.

Hash, Laura, in conversation with Corporal Gean Johnson.

Trefny, Dr. Frank (pathologist), in conversation with author.

Newspapers

Clinton Chronicle
Post and Courier
Press and Standard
Times and Democrat

Websites

DNA Forensics. http://www.dnaforensics.com.

"The M'Naghten Rule." FindLaw. criminal.findlaw.com.
State v. Blair. 176 S.C. 644 (1981). www.leagle.com.
Utah Department of Public Safety. forensicservices.utah.gov.

ABOUT THE AUTHOR

Lieutenant Rita Y. Shuler was a supervisory special agent of the Forensic Photography Department of the South Carolina Law Enforcement Division (SLED) for twenty-four and a half years. She interfaced with the attorney general's office, solicitors and investigators, providing photographic evidence assistance in the prosecution of thousands of criminal cases.

Her interest in photography started as a hobby at the age of nine with a Kodak Brownie camera.

Before her career as a forensic photographer, she worked in the medical field as a radiologic technologist for twelve years. Her interest in forensic science evolved when she X-rayed homicide victims to assist with criminal investigations.

Shuler received her basic police training and certification as a law enforcement officer for the state of South Carolina at the South Carolina Criminal Justice Academy in Columbia, South Carolina, and received her advanced specialized law enforcement photography training at the FBI Academy in Quantico, Virginia.

She holds a special love for the South Carolina Lowcountry and enjoys walking, beaching, crabbing, fishing and shark tooth hunting. She resides in Johns Island, South Carolina.

Visit us at
www.historypress.com